AF323412

THE MAGICAL CHANCE

THE MAGICAL CHANCE

BY

DALLAS LORE SHARP

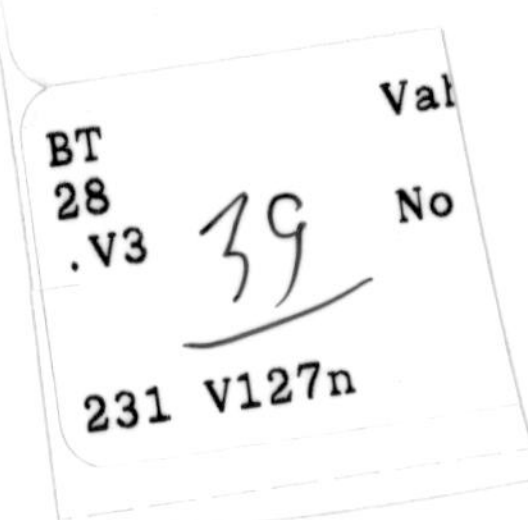

Essay Index Reprint Series

BOOKS FOR LIBRARIES PRESS
FREEPORT, NEW YORK

Reprinted 1971 by arrangement with
Waitstill H. Sharp

INTERNATIONAL STANDARD BOOK NUMBER:
0-8369-2133-X

LIBRARY OF CONGRESS CATALOG CARD NUMBER:
73-117842

PRINTED IN THE UNITED STATES OF AMERICA

CONTENTS

THE MAGICAL CHANCE

∴

CHAPTER I

THE MAGICAL CHANCE

THE MAGICAL CHANCE

∴

CHAPTER I

THE MAGICAL CHANCE

"WHAT are you going to say to the college girls?" my pretty niece asked, as we motored down the valley. She was being graduated this spring, and the snowy dogwoods and the purple Judas-trees against the tender hillsides were not so fresh, nor half so full of bloom, as she. But they were gayer far than she.

"Don't tell them, uncle, how wonderful they are! How the world waits for them! Don't say it, uncle! I have heard that sort of talk for these four years, and here I am with nobody waiting for me; not fitted for anything; nothing to do; and as wonderful — as thirty cents!"

Poor thing!

A few days before, I had seen an interview with the President of Yale, in which the young writer said he had read in a book that all the great devices had been invented; all the new lands explored; all the great deeds done — all the adventure and romance forever gone from life, and that only bread and butter remain with the odds against a young man's getting much of the butter.

Poor thing!

Have I been living fifty years — in America? or fifty cycles in Cathay? I cannot still be young at fifty! nor can I be so old either as modern two-and-twenty! Youth is a dry tree, these days; a sad state — particularly youth bent with the burden of an A.B. degree. Out of my fifty-odd years of existence I have taught college youth for three-and-twenty, and never in all that time have they looked like plain bread and butter to me. If they are not adventure and romance, not better stories, sweeter songs, mightier deeds than any yet recorded, then I am no judge of story matter and the stuff of epic song.

But my pretty niece declares that she also knows a shoat when she sees one; and she knows it is just pork. As for the college man of the interview: he was not speaking by the book; out, rather, of the depths of his heart.

It is an evil thing to be born young into an old world!

For the world seems very old. Its face is covered with doubt, its heart is only ashes of burned-out fires. The River of Life which John saw has dwindled into Spoon River; and his Book of Life is now a novel, piddling and prurient. But John also saw the Scarlet Woman — and that was long ago! The world was ever much the same; ever in need of an Apocalypse; and never more in need than now. My pretty niece, and the young man of the interview, are the world, and the college world at that, the more's the pity. They are its skepticism, its materialism, its conventionalism, its fear and failure. They seem afraid to bid on life, for fear it might be knocked off to them at something above par! They do not dare. They won't take a chance. They would, of course, if there *were* chances; they would dare, if only one giant were still left stalking through the land. The giants are gone!

The orator was celebrating the hundredth anniversary of Richard Henry Dana, the author of "Two Years Before the Mast":

> Life offered him a magical human chance and he ok it. There was something in him for which the ecorous and conventional life of Boston allowed no place in its scheme. "Two Years Before the Mast" belongs to the Literature of Escape.

Life offered him a magical chance — as if he were a special case! So he was. So is every boy. Who was this boy? and what were the circumstances under which Life offered him this magical chance? He was a Bostonian to begin with, and that is bad enough; he was a Harvard undergraduate also, which still further complicates the situation; and, besides, he was a Dana! Here was a complex which should have staggered Life. Who could escape from all of this? Leave that to Life. Up she comes boldly, just as if she expected the boy to take her offer. And he did take it. He fell ill with some affliction of the eyes; and, going down to the Boston wharfs, shipped as a common sailor before the mast in the little brig Pilgrim for a two years' trip around the Horn. And out of that escape from Boston and Harvard and the Danas, he brought back one of the three greatest sea stories in literature — a book that all of Boston and Harvard and the Danas combined could never have written except for this escape.

The question is: Does Life come along to-day, as then, and offer us, as it offered Dana, such a magical chance? Is there any escape for us?

We are not all Danas, and so we are certainly not worse off than he was; but our circumstances are distinctly different, and rather disquieting. This chance was given Dana far back in 1834, nearly one hundred years ago, when escape was possible, and when Dana was a boy. It was a young world a hundred years ago, and full of adventure. One could escape then because there was some place to escape into; but to round the Horn to-day is to land, not on wild Point Loma, but at San Diego, with the single exception of Monte Carlo, the most decorous and conventional city on the planet.

Perhaps my niece and the college boy of the interview are right.

About the time that Dana was escaping from Boston, a young man by the name of Henry David Thoreau tried to escape from Concord, of the same State. He had no deep-sea wharf, no brig like the Pilgrim, but, as one must seize such things as are at hand in an escape, Thoreau took a rowboat and the near-by river and started off. He rowed and rowed for a week, and came to Concord, New Hampshire. Here he took to his diary and wrote that there were no frontiers this way any longer. "This generation has come into the world fatally late for some enterprises. Go where we will on the surface of things, men have been there before us. We cannot have the pleasure of erecting the last house; that was long ago set up in the suburbs of Astoria City, and our boundaries have literally been run to the South Sea."

Born in 1817, more than a hundred years ago, and still born fatally late! How late, then, was I born? and you, my son? and you, my pretty niece?

"The rainbow comes and goes,
And lovely is the rose,

but you and I have missed the early glory that hath passed forever from the morning earth," she makes reply.

But I would say to her: It was ten years later,

ten whole years after Thoreau's tame adventure on the Merrimac, that gold was discovered in California. Here was a magical chance as late as the year 'Forty-Nine, and Life offered it to a young man of Providence and Brooklyn by the name of Bret Harte. He took it. There was something in him for which the decorous and conventional round of these cities allowed no place in their scheme. He went into the gold-fields and brought out "The Luck of Roaring Camp," another piece of the Literature of Escape. Then my students answer: "Yes, but there are no more outcasts in Poker Flat, and whom are we to write about?"

Alas, 'tis true, they're in their graves, that gentle race of gamblers. With the wind-flower and the violet they perished long ago, as literary material. Eighteen-Forty-Nine will be having its hundredth anniversary soon. But, some fifty years later, gold was struck again — this time on the Yukon. Here was another magical chance. And there was a young fellow walking the streets of Boston along with me, literally begging bread with me from editorial door to editorial door, by the name of Jack London.

Life came up to us and offered us this magical chance, and Jack took it, bringing out of the Yukon a story called "Building a Fire" which is surely a part of the immortal Literature of Escape.

"Well, what would he write about now?" they ask. "What has happened since?"

"Peary has found the North Pole," I reply.

"Yes, and Amundsen, or somebody, has found the South Pole!" they cry. "And what's the use of living in a world of only two poles, and some one finding both of them before we come along!"

There is something in that. It is a bad sort of world that has only two poles. It should be stuck full of poles, one for each of us. But there are only two, and a flag flies from each of them; as a flag flies over every terrestrial spot in between them: over Mount McKinley now; over the River of Doubt now, so that we are stopped from singing, as once we sang, —

> "There's one more river,
> There's one more river to cross."

There is no more river to cross. Theodore Roosevelt crossed it. There is nothing to cross;

no place to go where, on the surface of things, men have not been there before us. Yes, yes, there is Mount Everest. No one has yet stood on that peak; but there is an expedition climbing it, camping to-day at about twenty-five thousand feet up, with only two or three thousand feet more to go. And here we are in Hingham!

It looks bad. My young niece is possibly right, after all. East, west, north, south, where is a frontier? Where shall I go from here and find an escape?

Not overland any longer, for even Thoreau could find no frontier this way; and not by sea now, for here comes John Masefield, poet and sailor, saying the frontier has disappeared from off the sea; that the clipper ship, the ship of dreams, has foundered and gone down; that you can haunt the wharves these piping times of steam,

> "Yet never see those proud ones swaying home,
> With mainyards backed and bows acream with foam.
> . . . .
> As once, long since, when all the docks were filled
> With that sea beauty man has ceased to build."

Listen, now, for this is the message of the poem:

> "They mark our passage as a race of men,
> Earth will not see such ships again, —"

which makes me thank Heaven for my farm, where the same old romantic hoe remains about what it ever was — the first recorded wedding present.

Mr. Masefield's observations are dated 1912. Prior to that year real clipper ships rode the deep, and real romance. It was prior to 1839 that there were real frontiers and romance in the land, and a last house (a government lighthouse) still to be set up in the suburbs of Astoria City. Going a little farther back, we find that prior to 1491 (B.C.), about the year 4000 according to the margin of the King James Version, there were giants in the earth, and the stories in the Book of Genesis show that there were romances as well as giants in those days. But, like Thoreau and Masefield, Moses was born fatally late. I feel sorry for Moses and my niece.

Let us pause here for a sad brief moment in order to see just where Moses was when Life sought him out and proffered him a magical chance in the shape of a trip to Egypt. Where was Moses? and what was he doing? To begin with, he was keeping goats, a fairly common occupation in those days, though rather a rare job now. But that was not all: Moses was keeping these goats for Jethro, his father-in-law. Now you begin to get some inkling as to where Moses was. But this is not the worst of it: for Moses was keeping the goats for his father-in-law on "the *back* side of the desert." One would certainly say that the *front* side of any desert would be far enough away, and sterile enough of romance, if one had to keep one's father-in-law's goats there; but to keep the goats of your father-in-law on the *back* side of a desert is to be farther off than Hingham, or any place I know. And here was Moses when Life came upon him offering him an escape into Egypt.

He was born fatally late, Moses was, just like Thoreau and my niece. He might have been one of my own college men, so like a college man's was his answer!

"No, no!" he complained, "I don't want to go down to Egypt. There is nothing doing down in Egypt. I'm slow of speech; without imagination; and it's a hard job, anyway. Let me stay here and be goatherd to Jethro, my father-in-law, and dream of the good old days of the giants, when men began to multiply upon the face of the earth, when the sons of God saw the daughters of men that they were fair. Ah!—there was something doing in those days!"

From Moses to Masefield the times have been fatally late. And so mine are, with the clipper ships, the frontiers, the giants, and the daughters of men that are fair, all gone! But I seem to see them fair. I suppose I ought not, having been born so fatally late. And I wonder if I might not find a giant, too, if I should hunt? and a clipper ship? and a frontier? and even an escape from Hingham!

Lumber is still brought in boats to one of Hingham's old wharves, but the rest of her wharves are deserted. Her citizens, who used to do business in great waters, stop now in Hingham Harbor to catch smelts. Change and some decay one can see all about Hingham, but little chance of escape.

Down at the foot of Mullein Hill, on which my house stands, there runs a long, long trail awinding into that land of my dreams; but I ask: Where does it cross the frontier? I have traveled it, going south, in my Ford (if you are out for frontiers, take a Ford. We have a saying here in Hingham that a Ford will take a man anywhere — except into good society!) — I say I have gone south over this road which runs at the foot of Mullein Hill as far as Philadelphia, and no frontier! — the next stop was Chester. I have gone east over the same road until I came to within ten miles of Skowhegan, Maine, where I ran into a steam-roller on the road. When you meet a steam-roller on a road in Maine, you are very near the frontier. If there is any adventure for you on the trip, it will be on the détour around that steam-roller. But under the roller ran the road and on into Skowhegan, and on out of Skowhegan into Aroostook County, the richest county in the United States, where they raise "spuds" enough to feed, not only Boston, but the rest of dear old Ireland with her; and all the way from Hingham to Aroostook, except at the steam-roller, there was no chance to get off.

And this road, taking a turn among these glorious potato-fields of Maine, starts over the mountains of New Hampshire, crosses the corn and cattle belt in the central portion of the country, and, running on and on, dips into the Imperial Valley in far-off California, the hottest cultivated spot on earth. And all the way from Hingham, roundabout by Maine, to the Imperial Valley, you may not stop, unless you run out of "gas." And the oil companies do not intend this magical chance to attend you, for they have planted gasoline tanks under every second telegraph pole all the way.

This road, starting from Mullein Hill, Hingham, and running to Aroostook, Maine, and to the Imperial Valley in California, takes a new turn among the melon-fields there, works its way back along the Gulf States, binding their ragged edge like a selvage, and, bending into Florida, threads its way among the Everglades and out, heading off across the cotton-fields, on across the corn and cattle belt again, climbs Pike's Peak and down, climbs Mount Hood and down, and, faring on into the State of Washington, climbs the fruited slopes of old Tacoma, "The Mountain that was God." And all the way from Hingham some one has been there before us, and laid an oiled road for us, and left us no frontier.

Surely we are born late; and my pretty niece fatally late. The frontier is gone. The buffaloes are gone. I saw their ancient trails out of the car windows as my train roared over the Canadian prairie, wavering parallel paths in the virgin sod, a vivider green than the rest of the grass, narrow meandering lines vanishing short of the far-off horizon where hung a cloud not larger than a man's hand, like the dust of the last disappearing herd.

"Hank" Monk is gone. This king of overland stage-drivers sleeps in Carson City; and beside sleeps his Concord coach of split hickory. Concord has ceased to make such coaches.

> They mark our passage as a race of men,
> Earth will not see such coaches again.

From Hell Gate now to Golden Gate there are only miles, and any machine makes a mere holiday of the trip.

A young acquaintance of mine has just made the coast-to-coast run, driving her own car. She said to me on arriving here that "it was an awful monotonous journey." Didn't anything happen? I asked with considerable surprise. No, nothing happened. Didn't she see anything of interest? Wasn't there any excitement? Didn't she have any adventures? No, she didn't see anything; she didn't get a bit of excitement out of it; there wasn't any adventure; just one blinkety-blank mile after another!

"Incredible!" I cried.

"Oh, yes," she said, her eyes brightening, something like a thrill in her voice, "I did have three punctures!"

All the way from Golden Gate to Hell Gate with three punctures to break the cushioned tenor of her way. This is what life has come to.

Then she said: "There were two things on the trip that did greatly interest me. But I don't exactly know why; and I am afraid to tell you about them for fear you will think me such a big fool."

"No," I answered, "I won't think you any bigger fool than I do now, so what were the two interesting things?"

"Well," she began (and I wish the reader would note the strictly American touch in this description), "one of them was Luther Burbank's spineless cactus." (Notice, I say, the spineless quality of this cactus.)

The girl read my face and exclaimed, much hurt: "There! I knew you would poke fun at me."

"But tell what the other thing was," I begged. "Let's get the sordid story over as fast as we can."

"I don't know even yet what it all meant," she went on, "but, as I was crossing the Arizona desert, I saw a long petition being circulated by the native Arizonians, praying the National Congress to preserve for them and for posterity a portion of their original desert."

My poor niece! Moses saw the giants pass away; Thoreau saw the frontier pass away; Masefield sees the clipper ship pass away; but it remains for my niece and her day to see the Great American Desert wiped out by the irrigation ditch, and the gila monster with the desert, and the need of a shovel on the trip across the sands! Have we eaten the cassaba melon and gone mad? Is it all of life to make the desert blossom as the rose? To bring forth cassaba melons, and alligator pears, and spineless cacti for cow feed?

Ploughing the desert; turning the giant cactus

into ensilage, as if to live were a silo — for fear of this the native Arizonians are asking Congress that a portion of their original desert and of Life's adventure and romance be saved to them and to their children.

It is sad. But this is not the worst of it: for they have laid an oiled road across that desert, as if it were the whole of life to get through to San Diego on time.

There is no hope for a man who gets through to San Diego on time. He will strike Los Angeles on time, come to San Francisco on time. Portland on time, Winnipeg, Chicago, Boston, and Hingham on time; where he will die on time, be buried on time, rise on time, and keep going on time, with never a chance to get off. But where is the adventure in that? It is not the whole of life to get through to San Diego on time. I had rather leave my bones to bleach beneath a bush than travel on and on by schedule, always making life's connections, and so missing always life's magical chances. Don't you remember your Mother Goose, wise old dear?

"A dillar a dollar,
A ten-o'clock scholar,

> Why have you come so soon?
> You used to come at ten o'clock,
> But now you come at noon."

And he was the only little duffer in the whole school to get a poem written to him. The other children came on time and passed into oblivion; this boy (he certainly was a boy) came late and has become immortal.

The desert is doomed, no doubt, but we shall always have détours; and if "on the surface of things men have been there before us," we must go beneath. There are giants still in these days; the daughters of men are still fair; there are frontiers for those who will find them; and, clipper ships or no, I believe in the everlasting adventure of rounding the Horn. I believe in magical chances of escape, born though I was after my parents, which might have been fatally late had I not happily come before my children, each of whom is an adventure and an escape. Wherever I turn, I see a chance to sidestep the decorous, the conventional, the scheduled, to dodge into the bushes and escape. Every day is an adventure.

There are magical human chances to go round;

there is adventure and escape for everybody who will seize it. Youth is as young, the world as round, the earth as wild as ever. And, in spite of all those who have grown old, it is still appareled in celestial light — sunlight, starlight, moonlight — or else wrapped in ancient and adventurous dark. The sun still knoweth his going down, thank Heaven! There are some things that do not change nor pass away.

> Thou makest darkness, and it is night: wherein all the beasts of the forest do creep forth.
>
> The young lions roar after their prey, and seek their meat from God.
>
> The sun ariseth, they gather themselves together, and lay them down in their dens.
>
> Man goeth forth unto his work and to his labour until the evening.

Then look out for your men-folks. For this is the end of the decorous and conventional. This is the time wherein all the beasts of the forest do creep forth.

We are what we always were, and so are things what they always were, though they look different. We have changed the spots of a few leopards, the skins of a few Ethiopians, and shifted the frontier from the dark wild heart of the forest to the wild dark heart of the city; but we have not changed the darkness, or the wildness, or the Ethiopian, or the leopard.

I have seen the evening come over the city, a night deep with darkness and wild with a great storm blowing salty from the sea. I have watched the streets grow empty till the shadow feet of Midnight echoed as they passed, and all the doors were shut. Then I have crept down along the dark wet ways, bleak and steep-cut as cliffs, where I have heard the beating of great wings above the roofs, the call of wild shrill voices along the craggy covings, and the wash and splash of driving rains aslant the walls; I have tasted brine, spume, and spindrift on the level winds, flying through a city's streets from far at sea — "one-way" streets by day, and so clogged that traffic could barely move in that one way — but here — in the hushed tumult of the storm and night — I could hear the stones crying out of their walls, and the beams out of the timbers answering them; the very cobbles of the pavement having tongues that would speak when the din of the pounding hoofs was past.

Some one complained to Browning that Italy is

the only land of romance now left to us. The poet answered promptly, "I should like to include dear old Camberwell." And I should like to include dear old Haleyville and dear old Hingham. And you would like to include dear old Wig Lane, if you were born there.

But I started out from Hingham, pages back, to find the frontier. Have I found it yet? So Abraham started out from Ur of the Chaldees to find a frontier, which he called a "City without Foundations," and did he find it? Whether he did or not, he certainly had a plenty of adventure by the way. Abraham was a hundred years old when Isaac was born. There is something thrilling about that. Yet, narrow as that chance was, it is nothing when compared with what happened to him next. For, when Abraham was one hundred and *forty* years old, he married Keturah. Here was a man who would not be put down by a little circumstance like one hundred and forty years. Life comes along at one hundred and forty and offers Abraham Keturah, and he takes her!

I say he may not have found his city. We know that he did find Keturah — which is vastly more of an adventure. We may not have the pleasure of erecting the last house in the suburbs of Astoria City, as Thoreau says; but we might have the wilder adventure of living in it. And as it happens to be a government lighthouse out on Tongue Point, at the mouth of the Columbia; and as it happens to be where the night and the rain and the fog are thickest on the face of the globe, life in that last house is a constant frontier.

One might never leave Ur were he not seeking a city. And one must never find his city else he might cease his seeking. I do not know how old Abraham was when he set out from Ur of the Chaldees. I left Haleyville at the age of eight. I have only lately come to Hingham, having got in on the wrong side of the railroad track some twenty years ago. (If one is really to arrive in Hingham, one must come in with one's ancestors, and more than twenty years before.) I say, I was eight when I left Haleyville; that I have hardly yet arrived in Hingham; but all the way from Haleyville to Hingham, and all the way from Hingham to — Heaven, dare I say? — there has been, and there shall be, held out, in both of Life's hands to me, the magical chance of escape.

Did I start out from Hingham to find the frontier? That was wrong. I will start back for Hingham. Hingham *is* the frontier. So was Haleyville. So will Heaven be. Life with the earth goes round, not forward, except to complete a circuit established when the stars were fixed, an orbit that all the forces of Heaven and human intelligence have been unable to warp. The only variation or shadow of new turning Earth herself can look forward to is from collision with some mad comet, which, if she lasts long enough, may happen possibly within fifteen million years — a square head-on smash it may be, or only a side-swipe with a severe shaking up — and then fifteen million years more of steady turning. Things outside are rather hard and fast despite appearances, and we who are parts of this even scheme, we find that our uprisings and downsittings have never varied much from rule, nor are liable to.

We are, I repeat, what we always were, and so are things what they always were, though they look different. So is life what it always was for adventures and frontiers.

The wild frontier, like the hunted fox, has doubled on its trail, that is all. Romance has slipped out of the woods into the deeper places of the city; Adventure has turned commuter; and here are the three to companion life, as they ever have — the Athos, Porthos, and Aramis to a bebundled D'Artagnan. And already it is more than "Twenty Years Since."

Twenty years, or a hundred years —

"The year's at the spring."

If you do not find your fill of adventure with Davy Balfour in Appin, come down with him to Dean — to Edinburgh, and you shall see the face of such danger "in the midst of what they call the safety of a town" as may shake you, too, "beyond experience."

If you don't find the frontier in the daylight, wait for the dark. Every night is a fresh frontier. There are no landmarks of the day but are blotted out by the dark as the lines are sponged in the wake of a steamer's keel. On the shortest night of this year wild rabbits were in my garden, fox-hounds were baying beyond the quarries, and through the thin early mist of the dawn we were all at the window watching a wild doe behind the barn. She nipped the clover nervously, twitched her tail, pricked her ears (for the day was approaching), and took the high wire fence at a bound. She was as wild and free as the wind.

A few Sunday nights ago I was at church when the minister announced a series of evening sermons for young people, and, to my utter astonishment, his first talk was to be "Against Sowing Wild Oats." I was greatly tempted to ask him if he intended to prevent his young people from doing any more farming. If they couldn't sow wild oats, what kind of oats could they sow? Did he ever see any tame oats? Those preachers imagine a vain thing who think we ever cease to sow wild oats (at least, there is many a late crop, as Thackeray says). The truth is there are no oats but wild ones.

I do not know what seed catalogue you order your garden seeds out of; I get mine out of one marked "Honest Seeds"; it is assuring to have an order-book of this sort plainly stamped "honest" on the cover. In this honest-seed catalogue for the current year the seedsman, on page 56, is describing his oats. Let the preacher on wild oats note with critical care the terms of this description. There is something theological, at least, revivalistic, about them. It is the only oat described in the catalogue; and it would be the only oat to plant in all the world, if it were, as it is described, a "Regenerated Select Swedish Oat." A "regenerated" (that is Methodist) "select" (that is Presbyterian) oat! But read on through this catalogue, and you will find that every seed and tuber from artichoke to zinnia has been to a revival since last summer and hit the "sawdust trail." Great revivalists are the seedsmen! Their work, however, is not permanent. For they know, and we all know, that every regenerated select Swedish oat in their bins is a backslider at heart, as wild as the wild ass of the wilderness that scorneth the crying of the driver.

It is true of the seed and true of the soil in which it grows. This spring I brought in from the garden a frozen lump of earth which I had been subduing, after the fashion of Scripture, with my hoe, these twenty years. Nay, that lump of earth had been in process of being subdued for nigh two hundred years, here on this ancient Hingham farm. It was a bit of regenerated, select soil, which I had sweetened with lime, had nourished with nitrogen and potash, and had planted with nothing but regenerated, select seeds out of this honest catalogue. I put this lump of soil in a pot by a south window and tenderly planted more regenerated, select seeds within its breast — tomato seeds, Jewel, Earliana, and Bonny Best. Then I looked that it should bring forth tomato plants, and it brought forth within the pot, at the end of two weeks, pig-weed, horse-weed, chick-weed, smart-weed, white-weed, rag-weed, knot-weed, tumble-weed, milk-weed, silk-weed, sneeze-weed, poke-weed; goose-grass, crab-grass, witch-grass, wire-grass, spear-grass; burdock, sourdock, and *pusley;* to say nothing of the swarm of things from Europe, whose infant cotyledons looked innocent enough, but whose roots were altogether evil.

Life offered that lump of mother earth its magical chance and the lump took it. The innate badness of it, this cared-for, chemically pure, subdued piece of garden soil! Its frozen heart a very furnace of smouldering fires; its breast, that suckled the nursing salsify in the summer, a bed of such wild spores as would sow a world to weeds! Given tomato seeds, regenerated, select tomato seeds, Jewel, Earliana, and Bonny Best, the lump of earth brings forth its own original pig-weed, horse-weed, chick-weed, smart-weed, white-weed, rag-weed, knot-weed, tumble-weed, milk-weed, silk-weed, sneeze-weed, poke-weed; goose-grass, crab-grass, witch-grass, wire-grass, spear-grass; burdock, sourdock, and pusley. That is what it brought forth a million years ago. A million years from now, subdued and sweetened and nourished, and planted with regenerated, select tomato seed, Jewel, Earliana, and Bonny Best, and put in a pot in the sunshine of the south window, that lump of earth will bring forth pig-weed, horse-weed, chick-weed, smart-weed, white-weed, rag-weed, knot-weed, tumble-weed, milk-weed, silk-weed, sneeze-weed, poke-weed; goose-grass, crab-grass, witch-grass, wire-grass, spear-grass; burdock, sourdock, and pusley.

"The Form remains, the Function never dies;
While we, the brave, the mighty, and the wise,
We Men, who in our morn of youth defied
The elements, must vanish;"

— vanish, but not change. The heart of man is not less constant than a clod of earth.

"Lord, we are vile, conceived in sin,
And born unholy and unclean;
Sprung from the man, whose guilty fall
Corrupts his race and taints us all,"

— sings Watts with Augustine, with gusto and with more unction and consolation to me than in any other of his hymns. To know that we still inherit a portion of the original Adam, if only the naughty of him, is tremendously heartening. Anything original, if only original sin, in this day of the decorous and the conventional, is stimulating. For, if we do still come by all of Adam's original badness, do we not, by the same token, come by all of his original goodness, and are we not then wholly original, as the original Adam? We must be; as surely as the clod is; full, like the clod of wild weed-seed, and capable, like the clod, under the proper care, of producing tomato plants: Jewel, Earliana, and Bonny Best, regenerate and select.

I say the heart of a man is of the same steady stuff as the other clay. What it was, it is, and will be — wild, and ever seeking an escape from the decorous, the conventional, the routine of his subdued and ordered round.

How constant the heart of nature is to itself I saw again the other day at Walden Pond. Almost half a century before I came to this planet, Thoreau wrote of Walden Pond: "But since I left those shores the woodchoppers have still further laid them waste, and now for many a year there will be no more rambling through the aisles of the wood, with occasional vistas through which you see the water." Those many years have long since come and gone. Thoreau is gone; his cabin is gone; and a cairn of stones marks the spot where it stood. Over the stumps he saw, tall stranger trees now stand; and once more there is rambling through their shadowy aisles, and vistas through which you catch glimpses of the beloved face of Walden, calm and pure as when he last looked upon it.

"Why, here is Walden!" I hear him exclaim, "the same woodland lake that I discovered so many years ago; where a forest was cut down last winter another is springing up by its shore as lusty as ever; the same thought is welling up to its surface as was then; it is the same liquid joy and happiness to itself and its maker, aye" — and it has now been set aside as a reservation that its liquid joy and happiness may be ours forever.

Change is constant, but it is the change of the ever-returning wheel. Thoreau's cabin is gone, and no other cabin can now be built on the shores of Walden Pond. But the trees have come back to stay, and if, "on the surface of things" Thoreau "has been there before us," we must go below or above the surface and find our frontier.

"Magical chances?" a young aviator on the Pacific Coast wrote lately. "I thought of them to-day as I flirted with a little bunch of cotton-wool clouds eight thousand five hundred feet above Point Loma. And I wondered what Dana would have thought had one of his shipmates sauntered across the deck of the Pilgrim, and, clapping him on the back, said: 'I'll meet you, old man, in fifteen minutes up there in that fleet of little clouds; if they whift and drift into space, wait for me at the five-thousand-foot altitude'?"

So the frontier comes back. Pushed past the suburbs of Astoria City into the Pacific, it is seen crawling out on the sandy shores of Cape Cod with the next great storm. The single line of human footsteps across the polar snows has not left too packed and plain a trail. New snows have covered it, as new trees have shadowed the shores of Walden.

Peary's footprints, and Dr. Cook's, too, would be very hard to follow.

It was more than twenty-five years ago that I started from Savannah over the old stage-road to Augusta, finding my way by faint uncertain blazings on the tree-trunks through a hundred and thirty-odd miles of swamp. They were solemn miles. Trees thicker than my body grew in the ruts where wheels had run; more than once the great diamond rattlesnake coiled in my path, chilling the silence of the river bottoms with his shivering whirr. Once I heard the gobble of the wild turkey and the scream of the bobcat; and at night, while sleeping in an old abandoned church on the river bluff, I was awakened by the snuffling of a bear which had thrust its muzzle underneath the church door in the foot-worn hollow of the sill.

It was a lonesome place. A faint road led away from it off through the swamp; but, aside from the gravestones near by, there were no other human signs around. How long since human feet had crossed the threshold, I do not know.

The chintz altar-cloth that I tried to draw over me (the night was chill) crumbled at my touch and drifted off into a million dusty fragments. I had meant no desecration. I was very weary and had crept in through a window from the night and cold. A slow rain had settled down with the dusk, attended by darkness indescribably profound. And beneath the long-draped pines outside slept those whose feet had worn the threshold — slept undisturbed by the soughing of the wind, wrapped in the unutterable loneliness of the coiling river and the silent, somber swamp.

Yet here had passed a highway between two great cities just a few years earlier, before the railroad was built farther out through the State. Already the swamp and the river had taken the highway for their own, and from human feet given it again to adventure, to the gliding form, the swift wing, and the soft padded foot.

The giants of old, the frontiers and clipper ships of old, are gone. They went out with the ebb tide, and here already comes back the flood! And with it the same old human chance, the magical chance of escape. Lay aside the rifle and you pick up the camera — to creep with it into the lion's den; or to climb with it into the top of a towering oak, on some sheer mountain wall; and, pushing it before you along a horizontal limb, feet dangling in space, a stiff wind blowing, eagles screaming overhead, canyon wall below you, and far, far down the narrow canyon bottom, you hold on, body balancing camera, but nothing over against the swaying brain, and grind out a hundred feet of movie film. This is to shoot a good many lions.

Life offers us all the chance of escape. Go where we will on the surface of things, men have been there before us; but beneath the surface we need go no deeper than our own hearts to find a frontier, and that adventurous something for which the decorous and conventional allows no place in its scheme.

CHAPTER II

THE RADIUM OF ROMANCE

CHAPTER II

THE RADIUM OF ROMANCE

"Why thus longing, thus forever sighing?"

BECAUSE, I suppose, there were once two sides to her bread-board, both of which she used for sketching. She brought the board from the Fine Arts room at college to her new home, carrying it one day to the kitchen to try her hand at modeling — in dough. There are several of her early sketches about the house, of that period prior to the dough, which show real talent. Her bread, however, had about it the touch of genius. The loaves grew larger all the time, the bakings more frequent. The walls of any house are rather quickly covered with pictures, but there is no bottom to the bread-box. There are still two sides to her bread-board, and she uses both sides for dough.

"Why thus longing, thus forever sighing?
For the far-off, unattained and dim?"

Because, I suppose, time was when I thought of other things than the price of flour; not because of much money in those times, but because she made angel-cake most of the time then, and what bread we did eat was had of the baker; and because the price of flour was then a matter of course. The price of flour now is a good deal more than a matter of course, and the price of corn-meal even more than the price of flour; so that we must count the slices now, and cut them thin.

We shall have angel-cake again, I promise the children, with the biggest kind of a hole in the middle, giving them a bran muffin to munch meanwhile, and wondering in my heart if this fight for bread will ever end in angel-cake.

One can live on potatoes and bran muffins, although there was never any romance about them, not even during the Great War when Wall Street took them as collateral. We need cake. I don't remember that I ever lacked potatoes as a child, but, as a child, I do remember dancing while the pickaninnies sang,

"Mammy gwine make some short'nin', short'nin',
Mammy gwine make some short'nin' cake.
Ay lak short'nin', short'nin', short'nin',
Ay lak short'nin', short'nin' cake,"

in an ecstasy of pure delight, which was not remotely induced by common hunger.

Short'nin' cake, angel-cake, floating island, coffee jelly — are they not victuals *spirituels*, drifted deep with frosting, honeyed over with an amber-beaded sweat, with melting sweetness, insubstantial, impalpable, ethereal, that vanish into the brain, that thrill along the nerves, feeding not the body, not the mind, nor yet the spirit, for these are but three of our four elements — we are also the stuff that dreams are made of, and we cannot wholly subsist on more material fare.

What makes pie pie is its four-and-twenty-blackbirds. Singing-blackbird pie is the only pie, whether you make it of apples or rhubarb or custard or squash, with one crust or two. He dreamed a dream who made the original pie. And even now I cannot pass a baker in apron and paper cap without a sense of frostings and méringues — of the white of life separated from the yolk of life and stirred into a dream. I find the same touch of romance on many faces, both young and old, as I find it over the landscape at dusk and dawn, and on certain days even at high noon.

It was so this morning when a flock of migrating bluebirds went over, calling down to me. They came out of the dawn, hovered idly over the barn and the tops of the cedars in the pasture, then faded into the blue about them and beyond them, where a fleet of great white clouds was drifting slowly far off to the south. But their plaintive voices floating down to me I still hear calling, with more yearning than a man, perhaps, should allow himself to know. For at the first sip of such sweet misery some poet chides,

> "Why thus longing, thus forever sighing
> For the far-off, unattained and dim,
> While the beautiful, all about us lying,
> Offers up its low perpetual hymn?"

As if longing were a weakness and not the heart's hope; and our sighing — Shall I sigh for what I have? Or stop sighing? Some of my possessions I may well sigh over, but there are very few to sigh for, seeing none of them are farther off than the barn or the line fence, except a few books that I have lent my friends, and now and then a few dollars.

And such is the magic in the morning light that I see the beautiful all about me lying —

in the bend of the road, on the sweep of the meadow, across the commonplace dooryard asleep in the sun; and such is the sweet silence of the autumn day that I hear the low perpetual hymn — in the lingering notes of the bluebirds, in the strumming of the crickets, in the curving stems of the goldenrods, the loud humming of the aster-dusted bees, even in the wavering red leaves of the maples singing in their fall.

It lacks an hour of mail-time, and the newspaper, and the world. The bluebirds are leaving before the mail-man comes, and everything with wings is flying with them, or is poised for flight as if there were no world, except a world for wings.

The day is warm, with little breezes on the wing, hardly larger than swallows. They stir the grasses of the knoll, and race with them up the slope, to fly on over the wavy crest, following the bluebirds off toward the deep-sea spaces among the drifting clouds. And the curving knoll itself is in motion, a yellow-brown billow heaving against the moving clouds where they ride along the sky. And over the knoll sweep the hawking swallows, white bellies and brown and glinting steel-blue backs aflash in the sun. Winging swallows, winging seeds, winging winds, winging clouds and spheres, and my own soul winging away into the beckoning blue where the bluebirds have gone!

But I shall return — to the mail-box on this rural free delivery route, to the newspaper, to the tariff, to the Turk. The Democratic State Committee is assembled this day in Springfield. I am not there. I also ran. I stumped the State for nomination to the National Senate, and landed here on Mullein Hill, Hingham. Here I set out. Through many years I have developed the safe habit of returning here. It was a magical chance Life offered me; a dream of beating the protective tariff devils. But Mullein Hill is clothed with dreams; and magical chances make this their stopping-place.

It is certainly true to-day. To begin with, I have this day bought the field by the side of my house. For all the twenty years of my living here I have dreamed of this rolling field with its pines and pointed cedars, and rounded knoll against the sky. Not every day in the autumn is like this for dreams; not many of them in all the year. I shall be building fences about the field now for many days; and paying taxes on the field every day from this time on. There are not many autumn days like this for dreams. Yet to know one such day, one touched with this golden melancholy, this sweet unrest and yearning, should it not outlast the noon, is to know,

> "And one thing more that may not be,
> Old earth were fair enough for me."

You say that I am still thinking of the United States Senate. Possibly. "One thing more that may not be" I must be thinking on, for we all are. After the nomination comes the election; and what chance has the sworn enemy of a high protective tariff of election in Massachusetts?

Old Earth is fair enough for me ordinarily, and she is passing fair to-day. But even the dog, for all his appetite and growing years, is not always satisfied with bread and play. He clings closer than ever to me, as if sometimes frightened at inner voices calling him, which, like deep waters, seem to widen between us, and which no love, though pure and immeasurable, may be able to cross. He is nothing uncommon as a dog, except in the size of his spirit and the quality of his love. He will tackle anything, from a railroad train to a buzzing bumble-bee, that he imagines has intentions inimical to me; and there is nothing on the move, either coming or going, quite innocent of such intentions. Without fear, or awe, or law, he wears his collar, and his license number, 66, but not as a sign of bondage, for that sign he wears all over his alert and fearless front. He growls in his sleep before the fire at ghosts of things that have designs against the house; he risks his life all day long.

But he reserves a portion of his soul. He will deliberately chew off his leash at night, and, making sure that nothing stirs about the helpless house, will steal away to the woods, where he hears the baying of some spectral pack down the forest's high-arched halls. I do not know what the little cross-bred terrier is hunting along the frosted paths — fox or rabbit or wild mice; I cannot run the cold trails that are so warm to his nose; but far ahead of his nose lope two panting hearts, his and mine, following the Gleam.

All dogs are dreamers, travelers by twilight,

who wander toward a slow deferring dawn. They cannot see in the white fire of noon. A lovelier light, diffused and dim with dusk, is in the eyes of dogs and all dumb creatures, through which they watch a world of shadows moving with them like lantern-lighted shapes at night upon a wall.

> "Not of the sunlight,
> Not of the moonlight,
> Not of the starlight,"

is the tender, troubled light in the eyes of dogs.

There is a deposit, an infinitesimal deposit, it may be, of the radium of romance in the slag of all souls. Call it by other names — optimism, idealism, religion — you still leave it undefined; an inherent, essential element, harder to separate from the spiritual dross of us than radium from its carnotite; a kind of atomic property of the spirit which breaks up its substance; which ionizes, energizes, and illumines it.

There may be souls that never knew its power, but I can hardly think there ever was a soul shut in a cave so darksome, that romance never entered with its touch of radiance, if only as

> "A little glooming light, much like a shade."

This is the light in the eyes of dogs, the light

that birds and bees follow, and the jellyfish steering round and round his course. Something like its quivering flame burns down in the green, dismal depths of the sea; down in the black subliminal depths; and on down in the heart of the world. For what other light is it, that guides the herring every spring, in from the ocean up Weymouth Back River? or the salmon in from the Pacific, up, high up the Columbia to the Snake, and higher up the Snake into the deep, dark gorges of the Imnaha?

It is now long past October, and where is the bluebird's mate of June? She has forgotten him, and is forgotten by him, but he has not forgotten his dream-of-her; for I saw him in the orchard, while southward bound, going in and out of the apple-tree holes, the lover still, the dream-of-her in his heart, holding over from the summer and coming to meet him ahead of her, down the winter, out of the coming spring.

The dog and you and I and even the humble toad are dreamers at heart, all of us, only we are deeper adream than they.

> "If nothing once, you nothing lose,
> For when you die you are the same,"

says Freneau to a flower. Yet the flowers are of the dust that I am made of, and they too are the stuff of dreams. And the toad under the kitchen-steps, what he knows of my heart! As if the unrequited pain of lovers, the sweetest, saddest things of poets, had always been his portion, and their vague melancholy the only measure of his tremulous twilight song. When the soft spring dusk has stolen into the young eyes of the day, as the first shadow of some sweet fear into the startled eyes of a girl, then out of the hush, quavering through the tender gloom,

"A voice, a mystery!"

From his earth-hole under the kitchen-steps I have known the toad, by dint of stretching and hitching up on chance stones, to get nine inches up, nine inches from the surface of the globe, up on the lowest of the steps! Yet it is given him to pipe a serenade in the gloaming that no other lover, bird or poet, ever quite equaled, even when he sang,

"I arise from dreams of thee
In the first sweet sleep of night."

Life is always a romance. There is fire in its heart, even in the three cold chambers of the toad's heart; and the light of the fire flickers fainter than the guttered candle before it will go out. This may not be "the true light"; yet it lighteth every man that cometh into the world, every man with a pen, and his brother with a hoe, though they comprehend it not. One of our poets has written of "The Man With The Hoe" and left the man out and put only the hoe in the poem. This poet has written more than he has hoed, I am sure; as the painter of "The Man with the Hoe" had painted more than he had hoed, I am sure. Here is a poet who sees no light at all in "The Man with the Hoe," because that poet has written more than he has hoed, which is to gather where he has not strawed. When a hoe looks as black as this to a pen, you will search the premises of the pen in vain for hoes. I hoe; I know men who hoe; and none of us knows Mr. Markham's scarecrow for ourself. Here a realist sees what another realist thought he saw; as if you could ever *see* life!

Life is not what the realist sees, but what the realist is and knows, plus what the man with the hoe is and knows; and he knows that, if chained to a pick instead of a hoe, down in the black pit of some Siberian mine, he could not work life out in the utter dark.

Realism, if not a distortion and a disease, is at best only a half-truth; and the realist, if more than a medical examiner for his district, is but the undertaker besides.

Whoever sings a true song, or pens the humblest plodding prose, whether of Achilles, son of Peleus, or of John Gilley, a milkman down in Maine, or of the toad, or of the bee, has essentially one story to tell, and must be a Homer, truly to tell it.

Here on my desk lies the story of John Gilley, and over in the next farmhouse lingers the unwritten story of another milkman, my neighbor, Joel Moore; and in the other neighbor-houses live like people — humble, humdrum country people, with their stories, which, if lighted with nothing but their own hovering gleam, would glow forever.

The next man I meet would make a book; for either he is, or he knows, a good-enough story, could I but come by the tale.

O. Henry, pacing the streets in an agony of fear at having run out of story-matter, is only a case of nerves. The one inexhaustible supply of matter in the Universe that is of use to man is story-matter; for, as the first human pair have been a perpetual song and story, so the last pair shall be the theme for some recording angel, or else they will leave a diary.

The real ill with literature is writer's cramp, an inability to seize the story, all of it, its truth as well as its facts — an ill, not of too much observation, but of too little imagination. Art does not watch life and record it. Art loves life and creates it.

"No one knows the stars," says Stevenson, "who has not slept, as the French happily put it, *à la belle étoile*. He may know all their names, and distances, and magnitudes, and yet be ignorant of what alone concerns mankind, their serene and gladsome influence on the mind."

Art and literature have turned scientist of late, as if our magnitudes, names, and distances, as if the concern of psychologists, physiologists, ethnologists, criminologists, and pathologists, were the concern of mankind! These things all belong to the specialists.

What does mankind reck of the revolution of

the node and apsides? that Neptune's line of apsides completes its revolution in 540,000 years? Instead of an astronomer, mankind is still the simple shepherd, keeping watch by night, and all he knows of the stars is that they brood above the sleeping hills, and now and then, in some holy hush, they sing together.

Science is concerned with the names, distances, and magnitudes of the stars; and with problems touching the "intestinal parasites of the flea." Art, literature, and religion are concerned only with mankind; with the elemental, the universal, the eternal; with the dream, the defeat, the romance of life.

I have much to do with writers — with great writers, could they only think of something to write about. "There is nothing left," they cry, "to write about." "But here am I. Take me," I answer. Out come pads and pencils flying. There is hard looking at me for a moment. Then a cynical smile. I won't do. Becky might have done, but Thackeray got her; just as some one has got everybody! My tribe can never furnish her like again. Yet my tribe is not infertile; it is Thackeray's, rather, that has run out.

A sweet young thing in one of my extension courses, voicing the literary despair of the class in a poem called "The Fairy Door," made this end of the whole matter:

"The world seems black and ugly
When I shut the Fairy Door;
I want to go to Fairyland
And live forever more."

I was reading this effusion on my way in to college. When I reached the climax in the stanza,

"The world seems black and ugly"

I thrust the manuscript back into my bag in disgust and turned for relief to the morning paper. Here — for the young writer was the daughter of a prominent Bostonian — I saw the announcement of her engagement to a Chicago man, and I knew, of course, what ailed the poetry; and I knew the medicine that I should administer.

How far apart literature and life sometimes get! And how much more real and romantic is ordinary life than ordinary literature!

The girl was to meet me that afternoon in the university extension lecture. The amphitheater was full of city folk, and there in the middle of the hall sat the young poet. She was very pretty, one of the daughters of men still fair. Taking her poem, I read it aloud to that last stanza, when, turning sharply, and pointing the manuscript hard at her, I demanded,

"Is this so? Do you want to leave Boston for Fairyland, instead of Chicago? Do you?"

She was staggered by the suddenness and savageness of it all and rose to her feet, adorably pink in her confusion, stammering, "No, no, I beg — of course I — no, I don't" — by this time so recovered that her eyes flashed wrath as she dropped to her seat amid the gaping and the twittering of the class.

"If you don't mean it," I demanded, "why in the sacred name of literature did you write it? Why don't you ever write what you mean? And you mean that Boston has suddenly become a back number for literature; that the literary center has shifted to Chicago — that's what you mean. Chicago! the one romantic, fairy-like spot on earth! Isn't that what you mean? Then don't you see how fresh, how thrilling a theme you have in *your* Chicago?

No one else, perhaps, ever saw Chicago in quite this rosy, romantic light before."

Hers is the enduring truth about Chicago; as against that set forth by Mr. Armour in "The Packers, the Private Car Lines, and the People." Here she was, herself the very stuff of the eternal in literature, and forced to Fairyland for something to write about! Sheer nonsense. One need not take the wings of the morning to the uttermost sea, or make one's bed in Hell for "copy." Chicago will do — or Boston — or even Hingham.

To be, if to be only a stock or a stone, beast or bird or man, is to be a story, while to be any one of my neighbors is to be an epic.

The day we moved out here, before our goods arrived, a strangely youthful pair, far on in the eighties, struggled up the hill from the old farm below to greet us. He was clad in overalls and topcoat, and she in flowers, overflowing from both her arms, and in wild confusion on the gayest Easter bonnet that ever bloomed.

"How do you do, neighbors!" she began, extending her armfuls of glorious mountain laurel; "Mr. White and I bring you the welcome of the Hingham Hills" — Mr. White's rough old hand grasping mine amid the blossoms.

"Why," I cried, "I didn't know the Hingham Hills could hold such a welcome. I have tramped the woods about here, but I never found a bunch of laurel."

"Ah, you didn't get into Valley Swamp! Mr. White and I will show you, won't we, Georgie? We know where odes hang on hawthorns, don't we? We are busy farmers, and you know what farming is; but we have never ploughed up our poetry-patch, have we, Georgie?"

They never had; nor much of their other ninety-six acres either —the whole farm a joyous riot of free verse: fences without line or meter: cattle running where they liked; the farm kit — a mowing machine, a sulky plough, and a stolid old grindstone — straying romantically about the shy sweet fields.

It was an ode of a carriage that the spoony old couple went to town in, with wheels dactylic on one side and iambic on the other, and so broken a line for a back spring that Mrs. White would slide into Mr. White's lap without cæsura or even a punctuation mark to hinder.

I was at the village market one muddy March day, when Cupid and the old mare, neither wearing blinders, brought this chariot to the curb. Mr. White, descending to the street, reached up for Mrs. White, who, giving him both her hands, put out a dainty foot to the carriage-step and there poised, dismayed at the March mud. Instantly Mr. White, disengaging one hand, lifted a folded blanket from the seat, shot it grandly out across the mud, and with a bow as gallant as Sir Walter's own, handed the dear old shoes unblemished to the shop.

Eighteen or eighty, it is just the same. Boston or Chicago or Hingham, it is just the same. White or red or yellow or black, it is just the same. The radium of romance is mixed with the slag of all our souls. Here is my colored neighbor down toward the village.

"Hello!" I called to him over the telephone, "aren't you going to do that job for me?"

This neighbor is a most useful colored citizen, with a complete line of avocations, cleaning cesspools nocturnally and on Saturday afternoons being one of these sporadic and subsidiary callings.

"Hello!" he answered; "I most assuredly am! And exceedingly sorry I am, too, for this delay." (He had been coming for one year and six months now.) "But my business grows enormously. It is really more than I can administer. The fact is, professor, I must increase my equipment. I can't dip any longer. I am rapidly approaching the proportions of a pump."

"I am rapidly approaching the proportions of a pump." Divine! I like the sound. For it is the true measure of life as set over against that which life may merely appear to be. To trudge along through life beside your humble cart of the long-handled dipper, and to know that your dipper is approaching the proportions of a pump is to know that you are greater than you know.

I saw yesterday in the Sunday newspaper the lovely face of a girl, who, "rumor has it," ran the legend, "will be the next Queen of England." She, too, like my colored neighbor, like us all, is approaching the proportions of a pump. We are all the stuff that pumps and dreams are made of, and great art, and great literature.

I spoke of Joel Moore here in the next house

to me. For twenty-six years he was chained to a milk-route, covering Lovell's Corner, East Weymouth, and our back wood-road; but he always drove it in a trotting sulky.

From behind the bushes I have seen him calming the leg-weary team as it labored up the humps in the road, his feet braced, his arms extended to the slack lines, his eyes fixed on the Judge's Stand ahead, while he maneuvered against Ed Geers and Ben Hur and all the Weymouths for the pole.

He came home in that lumbering, rattling milk-cart as if it wore winged wheels, and were being drawn by the steeds of Aurora around the half-mile track at the great Brockton Fair.

It was sixteen years ago that Joel drove home with Flora IV, a black mare without a leg to stand on, but with a record of 2.12¾. There was large fixing of the little barn for her, and much rubbing-down of withers.

One day Joel was seen wandering over the knoll here near the house, kicking stones around. Something was the matter. I sauntered out toward my barn casually and called to him. Picking up a piece of rock in the pasture, he staggered with it to the fence, and fixing it into the wall, said with labored breath, "Flora IV has a foal!" And, lifting another stone off the wall, for ballast, he strode up the hill and over, and down to his barn, not knowing the "Magnificat," it may be, but singing it in his heart all the way down.

And this happened on the very hill which this day I bought with the field by the side of the house. Joel owned the field then. But he longed for a fast horse. I never set my heart on a fast horse; but I cannot resist a field. I did not covet this field of Joel's. I merely dreamed of it as part of my dooryard, and waited — longer than Jacob waited for Rachel. What a dream she must have been!

But let me come back to Joel and Flora and the foal.

My youngest boy was born that same summer — sixteen years ago — the double event in Joel's mind wearing the mixed complexion of twins. He had had no children till the colt came, and naturally he spoiled her. She was a willful little thing by inheritance, though — arch, skittish, and very pretty; and long before she wore shoes had got the petulant habit of kicking the siding off the barn at any delay of dinner.

She should have been broken by her second birthday, but Joel would take no risks; and in the third summer, though he "had her used to leather," he needed a steady old horse to hitch her with, and she came up to her fourth birthday untrained. Then, the first time he took her out, she behaved so badly, and cut herself so, forward, that it was necessary to turn her loose for months. Then she was sent away to be broken, but came back a little more willful than ever, and prettier than ever, if possible.

That winter Joel had to give up his milk-route on account of sickness, and with the opening of spring got the blacksmith to take the colt in hand. He took her, and threw her, dislocating her shoulder. Then he pulled off her new shoes, and she was put into the boxstall to get well.

After that, I don't know just why, but we talked of other things than the colt. She kicked a board off the back of the barn one day, sending a splinter whizzing past my head, but neither of us noticed it. She was seven years old now, a creature shaped for speed, but Joel was not strong enough to manage her, and a horse like this could so easily be harmed. In fact, he never harnessed her again.

I urged him from time to time, with what directness I dared, to let me take him into the hospital. But he had never left the farm and his wife alone overnight in all these years. Then one day he sent for me. He would go, he said, if I could arrange for him.

A March snow lay on the fields the day before he was to go, and all that day, at odd times, I would see him creeping like a shadow about his place: to the hen-coops, up to the line fence, out to the apple tree in the meadow, taking a last look at things. It was quite impossible for me to work that day.

The next morning the four boys, on their way to school, went down ahead of me to say good-bye. They filed in, shook hands bravely, fighting back their tears, and playing fine the game of bluff with him, though the little fellow, born the summer the colt was born, nearly spoiled it all. He is a dear impulsive child and had frankly been Joel's favorite.

"I've taken the eveners off the disk harrow," he was saying as he came out to the sleigh. "I gave the kittens a bed of fresh rowan. I drove a nail under the shutter of the can-house, where you can hang the key. You had better lock up a little till I get back" — his words half muffled under the big robes of the sleigh.

"I hate to leave home," he said, as we went along; "but she couldn't stand it. She's not well. It isn't so bad for me with you along."

Two or three times he was about to say something else, but felt too tired. I had him duly entered; introduced him to his surgeon; helped him to his cot, where a cheery nurse made him easy; then gave him my hand.

"Good-day," he said; "I'm going to pay you back some time. Only I can't." He clung a moment longer to me. "I've never had many of the luxuries. I've worked hard for all I've got — except for the little colt. She was thrown in. I never fed her a quart of grain — the cleanest little eater — as fat as butter — and on nothing but roughage all the time!"

Then, looking me straight in the eye, he said calmly, "You and I know and the doctors know.

But I couldn't tell her. You tell her. You can. And tell her I guess she had better sell the little colt."

He paused a moment. Something yet he wished to say — the thing he had tried before to say. I hope the Recording Angel took it down, and the *way* he said it, down. Not quite daring to look into my eyes, he asked, wistfully, "You don't need a fast horse yourself, of course, having your auto?"

"Yes, I do, Joel," I answered firmly; "I do need a fast horse. We all do, or something like that." And I bent over and kissed him, for his wife, and for my little boy at home.

There is balm in Gilead; but are there race-tracks in Heaven? — and fast horses there? Perhaps not. But I often wish that I had told Joel I believed there were. Of course there are. There is romance in Heaven, and the magical chance of escape there.

CHAPTER III

THE HUNT FOR "COPY"

CHAPTER III

THE HUNT FOR "COPY"

THERE never was a bigger, fatter, flabbier woodchuck than old Tubby — among wild animals that I alone have known. Tubby is a fixture of the farm. He was here when we came, or else it was his father or his grandfather. He is fat and flabby and as broad as he is long, and broader when full of beans. He is very much of a tub. When he sits in the garden, he sits like a tub. When he runs, he runs like a tub. And he holds beans like a tub.

It is worth a few beans to see him run — a medley in motions: up and down and round and round, the spinning of a top and the hop of a saucepan on a hot stove with amazing progress forward. He knows which end of him is head and which tail; but from a distance I can see neither head nor tail, only sides, bulging, tubby sides spilling down the garden. One seldom does see the ends of a thing from a distance. Tubby has a head-end; and he has wits in that end. He also has a tail-end; and the disturbing conclusion one reaches with close study is that Tubby has wits also in this end. He is a beautifully capable thing in his way. A cutworm is not more capable — if there is anything so capable as a cutworm! Both are poems; old Tubby an epic poem — were I as capable as Tubby, and a Homer —

A full-sized woodchuck is twenty-two inches long; and I presume that Tubby is not more than twenty-two inches wide, though I have seen him wobbling out of the garden and carrying off as mere ballast a cabbage or two, and a watermelon, and a peck or two of beans, and all of the Swiss chard in the three rows. There are several bushels of chard in three such rows.

The way he can run with his load! His little black heels twinkling through the vines, his shapeless carcass flopping into his hole with me on top of him! Then I will hear a chuckling deep down among the hickory roots, a peculiar vegetarian chuckle quite unlike a carnivorous growl. And then I will sit down on the hole and chuckle, having lost for the moment my carnivorous growl. He is so bold, so impudent, so canny. The old scamp rather likes me. And I am a fairly good gardener, if I do say it myself.

When I place a trap in one entrance to his burrow, he uses the other opening; if I put another trap here, he promptly digs a passage around it; if I block this with chunks of rock, he undermines the stones and patiently moves to a new house farther along the ridge; and, if I set traps for him here, he changes house again. It is a wide wooded ridge around the garden, and honeycombed with woodchuck holes. By and by he is back in his favorite house under the hickory — when the spiders have hung the doors with signs that the traps are gone

But it happened once that I forgot the traps. Wood-earth and bits of bark and dead leaves washed down till the wicked gins were covered, and Tubby, coming back after weeks off on the ridge, tumbled into one of the traps and got his thick fat fist fast. I heard him making a dreadful racket, and rushed up with a club in my thick fat fist.

Old Tubby stopped kicking and grunting, and looked at me. I don't believe that I was ever looked at by a woodchuck before. Stolid, sullen, defiant, there was much more of the puzzled, of the world-old wonder in the eyes gazing steadily into mine, as to what this situation and this moment meant. The snarled body was all fight and fear, but the blinking eyes sought mine for an answer to the riddle that I have asked of God. And all that I could answer was, "You fat-head!" And he said, "Fat-head yourself!" if ever a woodchuck spoke, and spoke the truth. "Fat-head, to set this rotten thing here and forget it!"

It was a rotten thing to do. Somehow he made me feel as if I had trapped one of my neighbors. He saw how I was feeling, and took advantage of me.

"Whose woods are these, anyway?" he asked. "Whose ancestors were here first, yours or mine? You didn't even come over in the Mayflower. But I came here in Noah's Ark."

"I know it. But keep quiet," I begged him, "and stop looking at me that way."

"What way?" he asked.

"Why, so much like my brother!" I exclaimed.

"But I am your brother," he retorted, "though I am ashamed to say it."

"Don't say it, then," I begged.

But he was wound up.

"Any man who is brute enough to set this sort of thing for his brother has no soul. And any man who can't share his beans with his brother doesn't deserve a soul. If I were as low-down and as lazy as you, I would go over to the north side of this hill and dig a deep hole, and crawl into it, and pull it in on top of me, I would." And all the time I was pressing down on the spring with my club, trying to free him. Suddenly there was a flop in the hole, and away in the sub-cellar, among the hickory roots, there was talk of me which I should have heard, had I been able to understand.

But I have much to learn. And so has Pup, our Scotch-Irish terrier. Time and time again Pup has sent the old woodchuck tumbling over himself for his hole. Once or twice they have come to blows at the mouth of the burrow, and Pup has come off with a limp or a hurt ear, but with only a mouthful of coarse reddish hair to growl over. He came off with a deep experience lately, and a greatly enhanced respect for woodchucks. But he is of stubborn stock. So is Tubby of stubborn stock. Pup knows that here is an enemy of the people, and that he must get him. He knows that Tubby is all hair and hide and bowels. He now knows that Tubby is deeper than he is broad, which makes him pretty deep.

The new light began to dawn on Pup when Tubby moved up from the woods to a corner of the ice-house near the barn. The impudence, the audacity of the thing stood Pup's hair on end, and he took to the blackberry-vines at the other corner of the ice-house to see what would happen.

Tubby's raiding hour was about five in the afternoon. At that hour the shadows of the ice-house and the barn lay wide across the mowing-field — the proper time and color for things to happen. And there in the close-cut field, as if he had come up out of a burrow, sat old Tubby, looking as big as a bear!

Pup stole softly out to meet him, moving over till he was between the chuck and the ice-house hole. It was a deliberate act and one of complete abandon. Things must this time be finished. And what a perfect bit of strategy it was! Hugging the ground when the chuck rose high on his haunches to reconnoiter, Pup would "freeze" till Tubby dropped down and went to feeding, then, gliding like a snake forward, he would flatten behind a stone or a tuft of grass, and work forward and wait.

The ground rose slightly to Pup's disadvantage, and he was maneuvering to avoid the uphill rush when Tubby heard something off in the woods and turned with a dash for his hole. It was head-on and terrific! And the utter shock of it, the moral shock, was more terrific! Neither knew for an instant just what had happened; the suddenness, the precision, the amazing boldness and quality of the attack putting Pup almost out of action. But it was precisely the jar old Tubby needed. Every flabby fiber of him was fight. The stub feet snapped into action; the chunk of a body shot forward, ramming Pup amidships, sending him to the bottom of the slope, Tubby slashing like a pirate with his terrible incisors.

But the touch of those long teeth brought

Pup short about. He likes the taste of pain. He is a son of battle. And in a moment like this he is possessed of more than common powers of body and soul. The fur flew; the grass flew; but there was scarcely a sound as the two fighters tumbled and tossed a single black-brown body like a ball of pain. They sprang apart and together again, whirled and dived and dodged as they closed, each trying for a hold which neither dared allow. But Pup got plenty of hair, choking, slippery hair, and leathery hide by the mouthful, while the twisting, snapping woodchuck cut holes in Pup's thin skin with teeth which would punch holes in sheet steel.

And Tubby was fighting with his head as well as with teeth and toes. He was cooler than Pup. He had a single-track mind, and it ran straight to his burrow. The head-work was perfectly clear; the whole powerful play going forward with the nicest calculation, mad as it appeared to be in the wild rough-and-tumble. There was method in Tubby's madness. He was fighting true to plan. But Pup was fighting to kill, and he lost his head. It was to win his hole, and life, and the pursuit of happiness on these ancestral acres that the woodchuck was fighting; and, as the two laid about them and rolled over and over, they kept rolling nearer and nearer to the ice-house and a burrow under the corner.

Over and over, right and left, they lunged when the woodchuck, sent spinning from Pup's foreleg, came up with the dog chopping at his stub nose, but, giving him all four of his mailed feet instead, he bounded from the face of the dog, and, with a lightning somersault, landed plop in his burrow, Pup raking the hair from the vanishing haunch.

And now Pup knows that there is no bottom to a woodchuck's burrow. But do I fully realize that there is no bottom to the woodchuck? I have been almost fatally slow over this lesson. Yet this is the writer's first and most important lesson, no matter what his theme.

"I have been studying the woodchuck all my life," said my old friend Burroughs to me, "and there is no getting to the bottom of him!" He made that great discovery early; eighty-four years of study confirmed it; and from early to late Burroughs never lacked for things to write about or failed of his urge to write. There was no bottom to his woodchuck.

Others have made this discovery concerning other things: the philosophers, of truth; the poets, of men and flowers; the prophets, of God. But the writer must find it true of all things, of all his own things, from woodchucks to God. There is nothing new in this discovery. It simply makes all things new to the discoverer. The skeptical, the shallow, the fool who says in his heart there is nothing but bowels to a woodchuck — what would he at four-and-eighty find at Woodchuck Lodge to write about? He might have all knowledge and a pen with which he could remove mountains, but, lacking wonder, that power to invest things with new and infinite significance, he would see no use in removing the mountains and turning them into steppes and pampas and peopled plains.

All creative work, whether by brush or pen or hoe, is somehow making mountains into men, out of the dust an image, in our own likeness created, in the likeness of God. It may be woodchuck dust, or dandelion dust, or the shining dust of stars; touched with a creative, interpreting pen the dust takes human shape and breathes a breath divine. A woodchuck pelt makes an excellent fur for a winter coat; the rest of him makes an excellent roast for a dinner; but it is what still remains, the wonder of him, which makes for sermon and for song.

How hard a lesson that has been for me to learn! And so slow have I been learning it that little time is left for me to preach or sing. If only I had known early that Mullein Hill was as good as Helicon; that the people of Hingham were as interesting as the people of Cranford; that Hingham has a natural history as rich and as varied as Selborne! My very friends have helped to mislead and hinder me: "I don't see what you find to write about up here!" they exclaim, looking out with commiseration over the landscape, as if Wellfleet or Washington or Wausau were better for books than Hingham! Hanover may be better for ducks than Scituate; but Hingham is as good as Hanover or Heaven for books.

One of my friends started for Hanover once for a day of hunting—but I will let him tell the story:

"We were on our way to Hanover, duck hunting," he said, "and at Assinippi took the left fork of the road and kept going. But was this left fork the right road? [An ancient doubt which had brought many a traveler before them to confusion and a halt.] It was early morning, raw and dark and damp. No one was stirring in the farmhouses straggling along the road, and we were turning to go back to the forks when the kitchen door of the near-by house opened and a gray-bearded man appeared with a milk-pail on his elbow.

"'Is this the road to Hanover?' we called.

"The man backed into the kitchen door, put down his milk-pail, came out again, carefully closing the door behind him, and started down the walk toward the front gate. He opened the gate, turned and latched it behind him as carefully as he had latched the kitchen door, and, stepping out into the road, approached our carryall. Looking up, then down the road intently, he hitched his right foot to the hub of our front wheel, spat precisely into the dust, and, fixing his face steadfastly toward Cape Cod, answered:

"'No.'

"'Say it with flowers!' snapped our driver, wheeling about for the other fork.

"At the turn I looked back. There stood our guide in the road, his right foot still in the air, I think; and there — though it is several years since, he may still be standing — one foot planted on the road to Scituate, the other foot resting on the hub of the wheel that should have been on the road to Hanover."

The man in the road knew that this road ran to Scituate. He lived on it. Had they asked him: "Master, which is the Great Commandment?" he had answered: "Take this road for Scituate." For were they not duck hunting in Hanover? Then what profounder error could they have been in than on the road to Scituate!

But most people go that way for Hanover. Every young writer I know hankers to get his Hanover ducks out of Scituate, as if, failing to get ducks, he might get Scituate; novelty, the mere novelty of gunning in Scituate when the ducks are in Hanover, making the best sort of "copy."

Is it some new thing that we should search

out, or some deeper, truer thing? Must we travel, or may we stay at home? Locomotion is certainly a curse to literature. No one nowadays stays long enough in his own place to know it and himself in it, which is about all that he can know well enough to express. Let the writer stay at home. Drummers, actors, circus-men, and Satan are free to go up and down the earth. And these seem to be writing most of our books.

For some years, now, I, also, have been going to and fro and up and down in the earth thinking that I might find some better place than Hingham. I have just returned from Wausau, Wisconsin, where they have a very hard red granite, and a deep green granite, both of them the loveliest tombstone stuff that, I think, I ever saw. Certainly they are superior to our seam-face Hingham granite for tombstones. Up to the time of my Wausau visit, I had never given much thought to tombstones; but it shows how one's thought expands with travel, and how easily Wausau may surpass Hingham, not alone in gravestones, but in other, even in literary, materials.

But Hingham has one thing in the line of

gravestones not found at all in Wausau: I mean the boulders, great roundish glacial boulders, gray granite boulders, old and gentle and mossy-grown, which lie strewn over our hilly pastures among the roses and the hardhack and the sweetfern, ready to be rolled to the tomb, and fit for any poet's tomb. When that shy spirit and bird-lover, Bradford Torrey, native of my neighbor town of Weymouth, died in far-off California, he left but a single simple request: that he be brought back to his birthplace for burial, and that a Weymouth boulder be found and rolled up to mark his grave. Were mine not Hingham boulders I would take one out of my wall, the one which serves as a gatepost, and, with a yoke of Weymouth oxen, would draw it to Bradford Torrey's tomb, a tribute from Hingham to Weymouth, and a gift out of the heart of one who knows and loves "The Foot-Path Way," "A Rambler's Lease," and "A World of Green Hills."

Perhaps one must needs go to California in order to come by this deep desire for Weymouth. Then let him go early. For if he is to write "The Natural History of Weymouth," or of Selborne, he must return early and stay a long time. Thoreau has been criticized for writing of Nature as if she were born and brought up in Concord. So she was. Can one not see all of the world out of the "Window in Thrums"? — that is, all of the world of Thrums, which is all of the world, and just the world, one goes to Thrums to see? "I have traveled a great deal in Concord," says Thoreau.

This brings me back to Hingham. I wish that I could write "The Natural History of Hingham"! A modest desire! There can never be another Gilbert White — but not for lack of birds and beasts in Hingham. Were I a novelist I would write a "Cranford" — and I could! I would call it "Hingham," not "Main Street," though that is the name of perhaps the longest street in Hingham. But there are many other streets in Hingham, and all kinds of interesting people.

And here I am on Mullein Hill, Hingham, with all of these streets, and all of these people, and woodchucks a plenty to write about — and planning this day a trip to California! I might have been the author of a recent book whose theme and sub-title read: "In the plains and the rolling country there is room for the individual to skip and frolic, but all the peaks are preempted." Come down from Mullein Hill; get out of Hingham; go West, young writer, as far as California; you shall find room to skip and frolic on the plains out there!

It may be true in California, but the opposite of that is true in Hingham. To be sure, I have tried to preëmpt Mullein Hill; I now own the knoll outside my study window, and the seven-acre woodlot beyond; but there are many other peaks here among the hills of Hingham, and scarcely any of them occupied. The people of Hingham all crowd into the plains. So did the people of Israel crowd into the plains — of Moab, leaving Pisgah to Moses, who found it very lonesome. There is no one on Pisgah now, I understand; no one on Ararat; no one on Popocatepetl; no one on the top of Vesuvius, nor on the peak of Everest, peaks as well known as White Plains or the Plains of Abraham, but not anything like so crowded. Moses sleeps on Nebo, yet no man knows where he lies. Have them lay you in Sleepy Hollow if you wish your friends and neighbors to crowd in close and keep you company.

Why has there been no Iliad of Hingham? There are Helens in Hingham, as there were Helens of Troy. Hingham is short of Homers. Mute, inglorious Miltons have we in Hingham. If one of them, however, should take his pen in hand, would he dream, and if he dreamed, would he dare to cry to the Heavenly Muse,

> "I thence
> Invoke thy aid to my adventurous song,
> That with no middle flight intends to soar
> Above the Aonian mount, while it pursues
> Things unattempted yet in prose or rhyme"?

Which of our poets thinks any more of an adventurous song? Of attempting any more the unattempted in either prose or rhyme? It is as if everything had been attempted; everything dared; everything accomplished — the peaks all preëmpted. Politics or religion or literature, it matters not: the great days are gone, the great things are done, the great men securely housed in the Hall of Fame. Heaven offers us a League of Nations and we prefer the tried and proved device of war; a famed evangelist comes to town, we build him a vast tabernacle, and twenty thousand gather for the quickening message — "Brighten the corner where you are!" And in the corners, and over the walls of the nation, with poster and placard the "Safety-First" sign warns us not to hold our little rushlight over-high, or flare it over-far, for fear we set our brightened corner of the world on fire. But the whole world *is* on fire! And wherever an emperor has escaped the devouring flame, he is fiddling, as emperors do; and his poet laureate is writing free verse; and all of his faithful subjects are saying, over and over, "Day by day, in every way, I am getting better and better."

"We are taught by great actions that the universe is the property of every individual in it," says Emerson. "Every rational creature has all nature for his dowry and estate. It is his, if he will. He may divest himself of it; he may creep into a corner, and abdicate his kingdom, as most men do, but he is entitled to the world by his constitution." I have not spoken lately with a man who seemed to think he was entitled to the world. That grand old faith has passed away. But I talk with no man lately who does not think he is entitled to an automobile. Great is Tin Lizzie of the Americans! Greater than Diana of the Ephesians. But except for our worship of the Ford we are not over-religious. The Ford is a useful little deity; she meets our needs to the last mile. The individual can skip and frolic with her, for she is distinctly the goddess of the plains and rolling country. Admirable to her winking tail-light, she is one hundred per cent American, the work of one of the supreme inventive geniuses of our time. She is the greatest thing in America, chugging everywhere but up Parnassus. Fool-proof, the universal car, she is the very sign and symbol of our antlike industry, the motor-minded expression of our internal-combustion age.

Even my quiet old friend Burroughs had his Ford. It was her creator himself who gave her to him. The creature would climb around the slopes and over the walls about Woodchuck Lodge like a side-hill gouger, Burroughs in his long white beard driving her, as Father Time might drive a merry-go-round. He nearly lost his life in her, too. But everybody nearly loses his life so nowadays; and nearly everybody had rather lose his life in a Ford than to drag out an endless existence in a buggy or on foot or in a wooden swing at home, watching the Fords go by. What is life, anyway? The Ford is cheap; the service station is everywhere; so, pile into the little old "bug" — on the hood and running-boards! "Let's go!"

Perhaps our machines are taking us — we wish to believe so — to some new Arden, some far-off Avalon, where we shall heal us of our motor-minds, our movie-nerves, our corner-light religion; where "Safety First" shall give place to "Derring-Do" as a national motto; where we shall ascend the empty peaks, and out of the thunder and smoke of shaking Sinai bring down some daring commandment, done by the finger of God on new tables of stone.

We are not lacking courage. It is imagination that we lack. We dare. But we do not think it worth while. We are shallow, skeptical, conventional, out of tune with the Infinite, and out of touch with spiritual things. If we do not try the unattempted, it is because we believe it has already been tried. It is because Homer has preëmpted Helicon that we tunnel it. Only Milton, among us moderns (and how ancient Milton seems!), only Milton in his blindness has seen that there is room and verge enough on Helicon, and deeps within the abyss of Hades where Dante would be lost. No, Milton is not the only modern to leave the plains, and, like a star, to dwell apart. Thoreau did it at Walden; Lanier did it on the marshes of Glynn; Burroughs did it at Woodchuck Lodge; and Hudson did it on the plains of Patagonia — proof enough that ponds and plains and the low-lying marsh may be as high as Helicon for poetry, if only the poet have the vision to see that

> "Like to the greatness of God is the greatness within
> The range of the marshes, the liberal marshes of Glynn."

But here we fail. We no longer see the greatness of God in things. We have covered God with an atom. We ask for bread, and Science gives us a stone; for God, and Science gives us an electron. It was a super-electron that created the heavens and the earth when it saw that all of the other electrons were without form and void. Atomism has taken the place of theism in our religion, if it is religion. Man is only a bunch of willful atoms, or parts of atoms, not any longer the crowning work of Creation, its center and circumference, its dominion and destiny and glory, its divine expression, interpretation, and immortal soul. Are we to be robbed of God? Inhibited forever from faith by the lensed eyes of Science?

"What is man?" I ask, and Science laughs and answers, "Electrons." That is its latest guess. But does man look like them? Does he feel like them? Does he behave like them? Does he believe like them? In the laboratory he may. But out here in the hills of Hingham, where I am returned to the earth and the sky and to my own soul, I know that I AM, and that I still hold to all of those first things which Science would shame me out of, offering me electrons instead!

I accept the electrons. Capering little deities, they are the sons of God. But so are you and I the sons of God — and we are electrons, trillions of electrons, if you like.

Gods and atoms, we can dwell and think and feel as either, the two realms distinct and far apart, the roads between in a continual state of construction, dangerous but passable. The anatomist, laying down his scalpel, cries, "Such knowledge is too wonderful for me. I am fearfully and wonderfully made!"—his science passing into poetry, and from poetry to religion, but not easily in our present frame and mood.

Science clears the sight and widens its range; but Science can never clear up the shadows at the bottom of a woodchuck. Only vision can do that, and Science lacks vision, using a microtome instead, paring its woodchuck till he is thinner than sliced sunlight before it can see through so much as a single stained cell of him. Science turns aside from shadows, walking by sight or else standing still. It deals with the flesh, not the spirit; and is as impotent in literature and art as in life and society. The potent thing among men and nations is love. Love never faileth. Yet never were we so afraid of love as we are to-day; and never did art and literature seem so fearful of the imagination, of vision, of the eternal, the divine.

"Go get me a bird," the old scientist said to me; "I will give you a lesson in skinning and mounting." I was a young boy. Hurrying out to the woods, I was soon back with a cuckoo. The face of the old scientist darkened. "You should not have killed this bird, it is the friend of man. See when I open this gizzard." And with a dexterous twist of his fingers turned inside out the gizzard, and showed it, like a piece of plush, its fleshy walls penetrated with millions of caterpillar hairs.

To this day I feel the wonder of that knowledge, and I thrill at the meaning of that bird's gizzard. Here was science and charity and poetry and religion. What untold good to man! What greater possible good to man? That was before I knew or understood the cuckoo's song. And neither the old scientist, nor yet his book, "Sixteen Weeks in Zoölogy," dealt with the song. Science is sure and beautiful with a gizzard. Poetry is sure and beautiful with both gizzard and song. And I wonder if the grinding gizzard or the singing throat is the better part of the cuckoo, even in this world of worms?

> "Though babbling only to the vale,
> Of sunshine and of flowers,
> Thou bringest unto me a tale
> Of visionary hours.

"Thrice welcome, darling of the Spring!
Even yet thou art to me
No bird, but an invisible thing,
A voice, a mystery;

"And I can listen to thee yet;
Can lie upon the plain
And listen, till I do beget
That golden time again.

"O blessed Bird! the earth we pace
Again appears to be
An unsubstantial faëry place,
That is fit home for thee!"

I have a great book, published by the Government, devoted entirely to birds' gizzards, mills of the gods, and their grindings. It is not a dull book, though the mills grind slowly and grind exceeding small. It is a book of bones, of broken beetles, seeds, hairs, feathers, and fragments. It is a great work of science. One might not like to lay it down unfinished; but, having finished it, one could hardly say:

"And I can listen to thee yet;
Can lie upon the plain
And listen, till I do beget
That golden time again.

"O blessed Bird! the earth we Pace
Again appears to be

> An unsubstantial faëry place,
> That is fit home for thee!"

Nature will not do, nor all the truth of nature, for stuff of song and story. As life is more than meat, so is literature more than life. Nature conforms to art; and in fiction "the only real people are those who never existed."

At Good-Will Farm, Maine, there is a rock marked with a copper plate. It had been marked for drill and dynamite, until, one day, my car swung up and over a sharp turn in the road before the schoolhouse, skidding rather horribly on the smooth outcropping ledge which had been uncovered and left as part of the roadbed.

"You ought to blast that thing out," I said, somewhat testily, to the supervisor who came out to greet me, my nerves, strung a bit too tight on the long day's drive, snapping with the skid here at the very end of the trip.

"I'll do it," he replied, apologetically. "I had intended to do it from the first."

The next day we were climbing this road on foot, and, standing on the ledge to take in the wide landscape of the Kennebec below us, I chanced to look down at my feet and saw, cut deep in the smooth surface of the stone, several parallel lines.

"Don't blast out this rock!" I exclaimed. "Tear down your schoolhouse rather. Build a new road through the grounds, but leave this stone. This is part of a great book."

"I don't understand," said the supervisor.

"Here is written a page of the greatest story ever penned. These lines were done by the hand of the glacier who came this way in the Ice Age. Don't blot it out. Put a fence about it, and a copper plate upon it, translating the story so that your students can read it and understand."

He did. There was no need of the fence; but he set the plate into the rock, telling of the Ice Age, how the glacier came down, ploughing out the valley of the Kennebec, rounding and smoothing this ledge, and inditing this manuscript for Good-Will Farm School ages later.

So much does the mere scratch of science enhance the virtue of a stone! Now add to your science history. Instead of the scratch of a glacier, let it be a chisel and a human hand, and let the marks be — "1620." Now read — if you can read and understand.

I copy it verbatim from a Freshman college theme:

PLYMOUTH ROCK

Plymouth Rock is situated in Plymouth Mass. It is the rock upon which the Mayflower landed in 1620. But it is not now where it was then. It was moved many years ago up to the street. And when they moved it it broke. But they cemented it together. It is four or five feet long; and three or four feet wide; and it is inscribed with the famous figures 1620, to celebrate the landing of the Puritans at that time. It is enclosed within a canopy of stone and an iron fence; but the gate is hardly ever closed. There are a great many famous stones in the world but this is as famous as any.

My mother was visiting me. She is a self-contained old Quaker, and this was the second time in all of her eighty years that she had even seen New England! What should we do first? What did she most desire to see? "Take me to see Plymouth Rock first," she said; and we were off, mother as excited and as lively as a girl. As we entered Plymouth, however, I noticed that mother had grown silent, and that her doctor-daughter, beside her on the back seat, always sensitive to her moods, was also silent.

We descended the hill to the harbor, came on in sight of the canopy over the Rock, and slowed down to stop. But the car had not stopped, when mother, the back door open, her foot on the running-board, was stepping off and through the open gate, where, falling on her knees, with tears running down her face, she kissed the blessed stone, her daughter calling, "O Mother, the germs! the germs!"

When Science and Religion thus clash, Science must give way. Mother knew as much about germs as her doctor-daughter. She had lived longer than her daughter; she had lost more, and had loved more — some things more than life itself.

Science has marked every rock; but only those that are wet with such tears and kissed with such lips are ripe for sermon and song. These are the eyes and these the lips of those, who, passing through Bacca, make it a well. Knowledge alone, though it course the very heavens, will come back to earth without so much as one shining fleck of stardust in its hair.

The other day a great astronomer was delivering a lecture in Boston on the stars. Wonder and awe held the audience as it traveled the stellar spaces with the help of the astounding pictures on the screen. The emotion was deep; the tension almost painful as the lecturer swept on and on through the unthinkable vast, when, coming to his close, he turned and asked lightly, "Now, what do you think of immortality? Is it anything more than the neurotic hope of a very insignificant mote in this immensity?"

The effect was terrific. The scientific smiled. The simple left the hall dazed and stunned. They lost all sense of time and space, they lost sight of the very stars in this swift, far fall. They had been carried up through the seven spheres to the very gate of heaven, then hurled to earth. The lecture failed — not of instruction, not of emotion, but of will, leaving the listeners powerless and undone. The lecturer may be right — for astronomy; and yet be quite wrong, for poetry. He may have uttered the last word — for science; but this end is only the beginning for religion.

How much greater an astronomer this college professor than that shepherd psalmist on the far-off Syrian hills! Ranging the same astral field as our scientist, sweeping the same stellar spaces, with only a shepherd's knowledge, the psalmist's thought takes the same turn as the scientist's, down to man, but on different wings, — the wings of poetry:

> "When I consider thy heavens,
> The work of thy fingers,
> The moon and the stars
> Which thou hast ordained;
> What is man, that thou art mindful of him?
> And the son of man, that thou visitest him?"

Then, swinging upward on those mighty wings, past the reach of science, out of the range of knowledge, up, up to the divinest height ever touched by human thought, the psalmist-astronomer cries impiously, exultantly,

> "For thou hast made him but little lower than God,
> And crownest him with glory and honor!"

This starts where the astronomer stopped. This is religion and literature. And I have these very stars over my hilltop here in Hingham!

CHAPTER IV

THE DUTY TO DIG

CHAPTER IV

THE DUTY TO DIG

I

A YOUNG man sat by the roadside, milking. And as he milked, one drove up in her limousine and stopped and said unto him:

"Young man, why are you not at the front?"

The young man milked on, for that was the thing to do. Then, with still more slackers in her voice, the woman said a second time unto him:

"Young man, why are you not at the front?"

"Because, ma'am, the milk is at this end," he answered.

And the chauffeur, throwing the clutch of the limousine into third speed ahead, drove off, thinking.

But the young man milking had already thought. To milk is to think. If "darning is premeditated poverty," then there is no saner occupation for human hands, none more thought-inducing, unless it be milking. Anyhow, when the Great War came on, I went over to a neighbor's and bought a cow; I made me a new milking-stool with spread sturdy legs; and I sat down to face the situation calmly, where I might see it steadily and whole. I had tried the professorial chair; I had tried the editorial chair; I had even tried that Siege Perilous, the high-backed, soft-seated chair of plush behind the pulpit. I may never preach again; but if I do, it will be on condition that I sit on a three-legged milking stool instead of on that upholstered pillowy throne of plush.

Whence cometh wisdom? and where is the place of understanding? The flaming flambeaux on the Public Library say, "The light is in here"; the Φ B K key in the middle of the professorial waistcoat says, "It is in here." But I say, let the flambeaux be replaced by round-headed stocking-darners, as the sign of premeditated poverty; and the dangling Key by a miniature milking-stool, as the symbol of the wisdom that knows which end of a cow to milk.

Not one of those students in the University who earned Φ B K last year knew how to milk, and only a few, I believe, of their professors.

One of these, with a Ph.D. from Germany, whose key had charmed his students across their whole college course, asked me what breed of cattle heifers were. Might not his teaching have been quite as practical, had there dangled from his watch-chain those four years, not this key to the catacombs of knowledge, but a little jeweled milking-stool?

I too might wear a key, especially as I came innocently by mine, having had one *thrust* upon me; still, as I was born on a farm, and grew up in the fields, and am likely to end my days as I have lived them, here in the woods, this Φ B K key does not fit the lock to the door of knowledge that opens widest to me.

I have read a little on the aorist tense, and on the Ygdrasyl tree; a little, I say, on many things, from the animal aardvark, here and there, to zythum, a soft drink of the ancient Egyptians, picking a few rusty locks with this skeleton key; but the doors that open wide at my approach are those to my house, my barn, and the unwithholding fields. I know the road home, clear to the end; I know profoundly to come in when it rains; and I move with absolute certainty to the right end of the cow when it is time to milk.

I am aware of a certain arrogance in this, a show of pride, and that unbottomed pomp of those who wear the Φ B K key dangling at their vests, — as if I could milk *any* cow! or might have in my barn the world's champion cow! I have only a grade Jersey in my barn; and as for milking heifers with their first calves — I *have* milked them. But breaking in a heifer is really a young man's job.

So I find myself at the middle of my years, stripped of outward signs, as I hope I am inwardly purged, of all vain shows of wisdom (quite too humble, truly!), falling in as unnaturally as the birds with the fool daylight-saving plan, the ways of the sun, who knoweth his going down, being quite good enough for me.

II

But how far run the ways of nature from the devious ways of men! The ways of Mullein Hill from the ways of a military camp! The Great War came and passed and left the earth a vast human grave. But through it all seedtime and harvest came to Mullein Hill, leaving only more and more abundant life. The Great War is an illustration on the grandest scale of what man, departing from the simple ways of nature, will do to man. War is the logic of our present way of living. I am not concerned with war in this book, but with the sources of life and literature. I have a cure for war, however, here on Mullein Hill; and this cure is the very elixir of life and literature.

War could have destroyed, but it did not change, my going or coming here in the hills. My garden went on as it had for years gone on. There was a little more of it, for there was more need in the village; there was a little larger yield of its reasonableness and joy and beans. But I did not plough up my front lawn for potatoes. Years before I had provided myself with a back yard, and got it into tilth for potatoes, keeping the front lawn green for the cow.

Though she is only a grade Jersey, the cow is a pretty creature, and gives a rural, ruminant touch to our approach, along with the lilacs and the hens. Hitched here on the front lawn the cow suggests economy, too. She is more than a wagon hitched to a star. She is a mowing-machine, and a rake and tedder, and a churn. The gods with her do my mowing, gather up and cure my hay, and turn it into cream.

Every cow gives some skim milk — which we need for the chickens, for cooking, and cottage cheese. Life is not all cream. If I speak of gods doing my chores, I will say they do not milk for me in the mornings, and that it is one of the boys who milks at night. A cow clipping your lawn is poetry and cream too, but caring for the creature is often skim milk and prose. Milking ought to be done regularly. Get a cow and you find her cud a kind of pendulum to all creation, the time to milk being synchronized twice daily to the stars.

I did not plant war-potatoes on my front lawn, partly because they would not grow there, and partly because, in times of peace, I had prepared for war-potatoes; and partly because I think a front lawn looks better in cows than in potatoes. If thou shouldst

> "So live, that when thy summons comes to join
> The innumerable caravan . . .
> Thou go not, like the quarry-slave at night,
> Scourged to his dungeon,"

— should we not all live so that, when war comes, we need not plough up the beds for potatoes where the portulaca and poppy ought to blow?

But what a confession here! When war comes! As if I expected war to come again! Many of us are fighting feebly against both the thought and the hideous thing. But many more are preparing for it. Our generals of the late war are going up and down the land preaching preparedness, as they always have. We learn nothing. They know everything. Their profession is war. Can a man lay down his life for a profession he does not believe in? The military men believe in war.

But so do we all as a people. War is the oldest, most honored profession in the world. In all of the fifty years of its history, the great University, of which, for almost half of that time, I have been a teacher, had never conferred an honorary degree. For fifty years it had carried a single laurel wreath in its hand to crown some honored head. Prophets came and went; poets came and went; scientists came and went; scholars came and went; but still the University, dedicated to life and learning, waited with its single wreath a yet more honorable brow.

Then came Foch, the professional soldier. Study for nearly ten thousand students was suspended; a holiday was proclaimed; a great assembly was called; and here, with speech and song and academic garb, with national colors mingling and waving palms, the laurel wreath was placed upon the soldier's brow. And this University, founded in the name of the Prince of Peace, dedicated to Christian life and learning, crowned the profession of arms as it can crown no other profession, and gave its highest sanction to bloody war.

I do not fail of gratitude to Foch. I only stand in horror that he is, and had to be. I would have had the Nation at the pier to meet him, but clothed in sackcloth, and every citizen with ashes on his head. I, too, would have suspended study and work everywhere for an hour; and, stretching crape across the Arctic Circle till the sign of mourning hid Matamoras and Cape Sable, I would have called an assembly of the continent, and begged this half of the hemisphere to cry, "O God, the foolishness and futility of war!"

The Duty to Dig is older than the practice of war. It was designed to prevent war; and to-day it is the only biological remedy certain to cure war. I must not stop here to explain its therapeutics as applied to war, for I am dealing with another theme. But just before the war broke upon the world, I wrote an editorial for a paper I was serving, advocating that a hive of my bees be sent to the German Emperor and one also to the war lord of Austria. I had extra hives for the British Prime Minister, the Tiger of France, Mr. William Randolph Hearst, and Mr. Theodore Roosevelt. If I could have interested these gentlemen, and a few others, in bee-keeping, I could save the world from war.

The editorial and the offer of bees were both rejected by the careful editor. "I must stay strictly neutral," was his timid excuse. At the very time I was writing, the Reverend Price Collier, a former Hingham preacher, was publishing a book called "Germany and the Germans," in which he set forth the old theory of military preparedness as a preventive of war. Speaking of the German army (this was in 1913), he says:

> It is the best all-round democratic university in the world; it is a necessary antidote for the physical lethargy of the German race; it is essential to discipline; it is a cement for holding Germany together; it gives a much-worried and many-times-beaten people confidence; the poverty of the great bulk of its officers keeps the level of social expenditure on a sensible scale; it offers a brilliant example, in a material age, of men scorning ease for the service of their country; it keeps the peace in Europe; and until there is a second coming of a Christ of pity and patience and peace, it is as good a substitute for that far-off divine event as puzzled man has to offer.

It is a minister of the Gospel who makes this profound observation. But it sounds like our present Secretary of War, a banker, and like our present Commanding General, a professional soldier. Here is sure proof that the human race cannot learn the essential things, and so, is doomed.

But I wish I might try my bees. This old hoax of preventing war by preparing men to fight has been so often tried! And we are at it again. But no nation has tried my simple and inexpensive substitute of bees and ploughshares, and pruning hooks. They have tried, from time out of memory, to beat their swords and spears into garden tools, but a sword makes a mighty poor ploughshare. It has never been successfully done. The manufacturing process is wrong. It takes the temper out of good garden steel first to heat it in the fires of war. We must reverse the process: turn the virgin metal into garden steel first, and give every man a hoe, and a ploughshare, and a pruning hook; then he will never have need for sword and spear.

III

INSTEAD of universal military training, I would advocate a hive of bees for everybody, or a backyard garden. A house should have both lawn and garden, even though the gooseberries crowd the house out to the roadside, where the human house instinctively edges to see the neighbors in their new pony-coats go by. Let my front door stand open; while over the back stoop the old-fashioned roses and the grape-vines draw a screen.

But give me a house with a yard rather than a hole in the wall, a city tenement, or a flat. The whole trend of society is toward the city, or camp, military, rather than agricultural. The modern city is a social camp. Life is becoming a series of mass movements, military maneuvers, at the command of social leaders. Industry has long been militarized both in form and spirit, and is rapidly perfecting its organization. To-day, 1923, there are more than a hundred different automobile manufacturing concerns in this country. Only those capable of "quantity production" will survive. Already the manufacturers see the entire industry reduced to five different concerns. This is strictly military, the making of society into a vast, and vaster machine, which, too great at last for control, will turn upon and crush its makers.

We are all conscripted. The Draft Board of industrialism allows no exemptions. The only way I see is to desert, to take to the woods, as I have done, to return individually to a simple, elemental manner of life out of the soil. But who can pay the social cost? Our social or camp psychology is better understood and more easily handled than the mind of the lone scout within us. We are gregarious by nature; we hunt in packs, we collect into crowds. Yet we are selves, separate, single, each of us a cave-man as well as cliff-dweller, a Remus as well as a Romulus. The city-building brother killed his country brother. And the murder still goes on.

Out of a commentary on the Bible I take the following observation, partly for its charm, but also because it holds a profound truth:

> God's people from the earliest time had never been builders of cities. The earliest account of city-building is that of the city of Enoch by Cain, and all the subsequent mention of city-building is in connection with the apostate families of the earth, such as Nimrod and his descendants, the Canaanites and the Egyptians. Sodom is one of the earliest mentioned cities properly so called, and the story of it is not encouraging for the people of God.

But which is the city whose story is encouraging to the people of God? Not Boston's, nor New York's, nor London's, nor Vienna's. Vienna is starving; the country is bankrupt; Austria's governmental machine is a total wreck; but the peasant goes his way, suffering little inconvenience, though the crown is not to-day worth the paper it is printed on. The peasant lives on the land, not on the bank; he gets his simple life directly out of the soil instead of a pay envelope; he has no New York, New Haven and Hartford stock, worth one hundred and eighty-six dollars yesterday, and ten dollars to-day, to-morrow, and until he starves. He has a piece of land and, impossible as it sounds on paper, lives on it, and out of it, and in it, an almost independent life, as the wage-slave and the coupon-victim cannot live.

We shall face a famine, so long as our door-yards are all lawn in front and all garbage-can behind. We have farmers enough — one to every eight of our population, I believe — who might produce sufficient raw potatoes; but Aroostook County is barely contiguous to the United States, and such a barrage of frost was laid down across its borders this last winter that, if one brought potatoes out of Aroostook between December and March, he had to bear them in his bosom.

Aroostook County is the greatest potato-patch in the world; the American imagination loves to hover over the tubered tracts of Aroostook, the *richest* county in the world; loves to feel that the world could be fed from Aroostook, were it not for the triple alliance of the cold and the contiguity and a railroad that runs, if not like a broken tooth, then like a foot out of joint, into these remote dreamlands of Maine.

Woe to them that go down to the railroads for help; and stay on engines and trust in empties, because they are many; and in officials, because they are very strong. Now the officials are men and not God, and their engines steel and not spirit. Why should a rational, spiritual human society trust its well-being to such paltry powers, when all the forces of nature are at its command?

I will put more trust in an acre of land than in a Continental Congress. I had rather have a hoe at my right hand than an army of bank presidents. Give me the rising and the setting sun, the four seasons, and the peasant's portion; and you may have the portion of the president.

I said we have farmers enough to raise all we need. We have more than enough. We have more than enough bankers; more than enough automobile-makers; more than enough storekeepers; more than enough coal-miners; more than enough cooks and janitors. But we have nowhere near enough landowners and peasants.

Nothing in the world would so straighten out society as to declare next year a Year of Jubilee, and give every man, not a job, but his birthright, a piece of land.

We are over-organized and almost de-individualized. But the time must again come when every man shall dig and every woman spin, and every family build its own automobile, distill its own petrol, and work out its taxes on the road. We shall always hold to the social principle of the division of labor — I plough for you; and you shoe my horse for me. But we have carried the principle, in our over-organization, to the point where a man's whole part in the world's work consists in putting on the left hind wheel of endless automobiles.

An eight-hour day will not save that man. And he is typical of all men to-day. Only by his acceptance of the duty to dig can he be saved, and society with him. The principle of the division of labor has been misapplied: instead of specialization and the narrowing of each man's portion, it should be applied broadly, multiplying his labors. Work is creative; it is self-expression; and I should let no man do for me what I can do. He robs me of living who robs me of doing.

The theory of present-day society — specialization, organization, combination, quantity production — is a fatal application of a perfectly sound principle. Six automobile combinations which in a year can destroy a hundred lesser combinations, can in another year destroy all but one of each other; and that remaining one, having nothing now to destroy, must turn and destroy itself.

IV

But I am concerned with life and literature. How does the organization of society affect books, admitting that it affects life? What is a book but a life? — and a more abundant life? Everybody who has lived has a book to write. But only those who have lived abundantly should write their books. Starve a nation spiritually, as ours is being starved; reduce its life to a mechanical routine; rob its labor of all creative quality, and how shall it write?

The duty to dig applies first to the spirit. There is sound economy in it if one's political economy is sound. I do not say money. Economy and money are not equivalent terms. I digged as a duty last year; and as a result I did not buy a potato from the "combine" in Maine; I nearly got on without a pound of beef from Chicago; and could have made my honey serve for Cuban sugar. The same amount of time spent putting left hind wheels on automobiles might have brought me more money, and so, more beef and potatoes and sugar, and so, more gout and rheumatism. The duty to dig comprehends a great deal more than ordinary economy.

I would not imply that I can handle the Beef Trust and the potato pirates and the sugar barons with my humble hoe; or snap my fingers in the face of Standard Oil, and say, "Go to, I'll have none of your twenty-eight-cent gas!" I do say that several million bee-keepers and potato-patchers, and hen-coopers, keeping busy in their back yards, as I keep busy in mine, could mightily relieve the railroad congestion, and save gasoline, and cut in on the demand for Chicago beef and cold-storage eggs, and generally lower the high cost of living.

It is not because there are "millions in it" that I would have the banker plant his back yard to beans. Thoreau planted two acres and a half to beans and potatoes (on a weak market, however), with a "pecuniary profit of $8.71½." Here is no very great financial inducement to a busy banker, or to a ward boss. Still, who better than the ward boss or the banker could afford a private beanfield?

I say it is not for the sake of this $8.71½ profit of Thoreau's that we must dig; but rather for that chapter on the bean field in Walden Pond, which proves the real worth of digging.

There can hardly be a form of labor so elemental, so all-demanding, so abundantly yielding of the fruits of life, as digging. Yet there are those who doubt the wisdom of digging because things can be bought cheaper at the store; and those who question their right to dig when they can hire a man to dig for them; and there are those who hate to dig, who contemn duty, who, if they plant, will plant a piece of fallow land with golf-balls only, and hoe it with brassies, niblicks, cleeks, and spooners, saying with Chaucer's Monk:

> "... how shall the world be servèd?
> Let Austyn have his swynk to him reservèd."

Golf is an ancient game, no doubt, but not so old as gardening, though golf's primordial club and vocabulary seem like things long left over, bits of that Missing-Link Period between our arboreal and cave-day past. Except for calling the cows from the meadow, or fighting in war, there is nothing we do that requires words and weapons, tools, instruments, implements, utensils, apparatus, machinery, or mechanisms so lacking in character and comeliness as the words and clubs of golf. The gurglings of infants seem articulate, even to unparental ears, compared with the jargon of golf; and as for billiard-cues, baseball-bats, pikes, spades, shillalahs, and teething-rings, they have the touch of poetry on them; whereas the golf-club was conceived and shaped in utter unimaginativeness.

Golf is not an ancient game: it has the mark of the Machine upon it; the Preadamites could not have figured the game out. Gardening, on the other hand, if we trust Holy Writ, was an institution founded before the Fall, incorporated with the social order from the start — an inherent, essential element in the constitution of human things:

> "Great nature's *primal* course,
> Chief nourisher in life's feast,"

— which civilization doth murder as Macbeth murdered sleep.

Golf belongs to civilization strictly, not to the human race, being one of life's post-Edenic precautions, like psychopathic hospitals, jails, and homes for the feeble-minded. A golf course is a little-wanderers' home; and if we must have golf courses, let their hazards be carefully constructed on worthless land, and let the Civil Service Board examine the caddies, whether they be fit guards for the golfers, lest some small boy be wasted who might have tended real sheep on Norfolk Downs or have weeded in a garden.

It is a duty to dig, to nail the Stars and Stripes to a lima-bean pole, and plant the banner square in the middle of the garden. Profits? pleasures? Both sorts will grow, especially the pleasures, which really are part of the profits, till they fairly smother the weeds; not the least of these being your sense of living and your right to live, which comes out of actually hoeing your own row — a literal row of beans or corn or tomatoes.

Somebody must feed the soldiers; but nobody must needs feed me. It is not necessary that I live, however necessary I find it to eat; eating, like sleeping and breathing and keeping warm, being strictly a private enterprise that nobody but I need see as necessary or be responsible for.

The soldier must carry a shovel nowadays, but he will require a hoe, too, and a pruning hook, and a ploughshare, before he will be self-supporting. With such a kit war could support war forever, which is the Rathenau plan of war, with everything German left out, consequently everything of war left out. The soldier cannot feed himself. The crew of a battleship cannot be expected to catch their own cod and flounders. They must leave that to the trawlers, those human boats, with human crews who fish for a living. Men of the navy must die for a living. The captain of a United States destroyer, writing to his wife, says, "I think that the only real anxiety is lest we may not get into the big game at all. I do not think that any of us are bloodthirsty or desirous of glory or advancement, but we have to justify our existence."

So does every human being; yet an existence that can be justified only by fighting and dying is too unproductive, too far from self-supporting, to warrant the sure calling and election of many of us. No Grand-Banker ever wrote so to his wife, though he might be returning with all his salt unwet; no college professor ever wrote so — not if he could get into his garden — in spite of his pupils, his college president, the trustees, and Mr. Carnegie's Efficiency Board. Teaching may not justify a professor's existence, though it ought to justify his salary; so, every time I start for the University, I put a dozen or two of eggs into my book-bag, that I may have a right to the tree of life, and may enter in through the gates into the city.

I am not independent of society. I do not wish to be independent. I wish to be debtor to all and have all debtors to me. But we buy too much and sell too much of life, and raise too little. We *pay* for all we get. Sometimes we get all we pay for, but not often; and if we never did, still life has so thoroughly adopted the business standard, that we had rather keep on paying than trying to grow our way.

Business is a way of living by proxy; money is society's proxy for every sort of implement and tool. To produce something, however — some actual wealth, a pennyweight of gold-dust, a pound of honey, a dozen eggs, a book, a boy, a bunch of beets; some real wealth out of the soil, out of my loins, out of my brains, out of my muscles and the sap of the maple, the rains and sunshine and the soil, out of the rich veins of the earth or the swarming waters of the sea — this is to be; and to be myself, and not a proxy, is to lose my life and save it, and to justify my existence.

I have to buy a multitude of things — transportation, coal, dentistry, news, flour, and clothes. I have paid in money for them. I have also paid in real wealth, having given, to balance my charge on society, an equivalent in raw cabbage, pure honey, fresh eggs, and the like, from my own created store. I am doubtless in debt to society, but I have tried to give wealth for wealth, not the symbol of it merely; and last year, as I balanced my books, I think the world was in debt to me by several bunches of beets. I do not boast of the beets, though they take me out of the debtor's prison where most of us live. I can face the world, however, with those beets; I have gone over the top, have done my bit, with beets.

The oldest duty on the human conscience is the duty to dig. I am a college teacher, and that is an honorable, if futile, profession. The Scriptures say: "He gave some, apostles; and some, prophets; and some, evangelists; and some, pastors and teachers"; but, before there were any such multifarious and highly specialized needs, it was said unto our first father: "Replenish the earth and subdue it" — a universal human need, a call to duty, from which no Draft Board of civilization can rightly exempt us.

Wealth is not created, not even increased, in trade. When was one pennyweight of gold on 'change by any magic metallurgy of trade made two pennyweight? The magic of the second pennyweight is the metallurgy of the pick and shovel and cradle rocking the shining sands of the Yukon. Real wealth is only circulated in trade. It comes from primal sources — from the gold-fields, the cotton-fields, the corn-fields, the fir-clad sides of Katahdin, the wide gray waters of the Grand Banks, the high valleys of the sheeped Sierras, and from back yards, like mine, that bring forth thirty- and sixty- and an hundred-fold.

And this is as profoundly true of life and literature as it is of cotton and lumber and gold.

Give me a garden and the wages of hoeing my row. And if not a garden, then a little house of hens, a coop of pigeons, a colony of bees — even in the city I should keep bees, if I had to keep them in the attic or on the roof. Not every one can have a garden, but every one can either plant a tree, or raise one pig, or keep a cow or goat, or feed a few hens, or raise a flock of pigeons, or do something that will bring him personally into contact with real things, and make it possible for him to help pay his way with real wealth, and in part, at least, to justify his existence, and his book.

CHAPTER V

THE MAN AND THE BOOK

CHAPTER V

THE MAN AND THE BOOK

HERE on my desk lies a new book entitled, "For the Benefit of My Creditors," the autobiography of Hinckley Gilbert Mitchell, a scholar, a teacher in a school of theology — and now this book, a simple, sad book of human struggle and defeat, of spiritual and scientific adventure and triumph and romance.

The scholar is not the accepted stuff of literature. What of human interest can come out of a classroom? Yet I have seen this scholar's classroom when it was wilder than ten nights in a barroom crowded into one. I have seen some lively and human times in my own classroom; and I know that there is as real a chance, and as magical a chance, there as Dana found on the high seas. There are frontiers for the scholar, especially in theology, as dangerous in their crossing as any to be met with by the overland pioneer.

Dana escaped from the decorous and the conventional life of social Boston by way of the deep sea; Mitchell escaped from the decorous and conventional dogma of his church by way of honest study; and his Church tried him for heresy, and found him guilty, and would have burned him at the stake had that been the decorous and conventional manner of dealing with heretics at the moment. As it was, they only branded him, and cast him out as a thing unclean.

Perhaps that is not a life human enough, and abundant enough, for a book. It is the simple story of a poor boy picking stones and building walls on his father's farm in New York State; then, as Director of the American School of Oriental Research in Jerusalem, rebuilding "The Wall of Nehemiah"; then, as scholar and professor, re-creating "The World before Abraham"; and finally, as the storm center of one of the bitterest theological controversies of recent years, dismissed, dishonored, betrayed for less than thirty pieces of silver, a silent, broken-hearted man. It is only another version of an old and very common story. Prophets and pioneers are all alike; and their stories are much alike, whether the pages turn westward, where new empires take their way, or eastward, back along the scholar's crossed and tangled trails to a world before Abraham.

As the manuscript of the book lay upon my table, I wondered if any publisher would feel the human pathos of the struggle, and the mighty meaning of it all for truth. Who would publish it? But here it is, printed and bound, a book — "For the Benefit of My Creditors," as if he were debtor to all, his enemies included, and owed them only love.

This is as modest and self-withholding a story as a man ever told of himself. There are all too few of such human stories. This one would never have been told had the author not hated intellectual cowardice as he hated moral cowardice, with a perfect hatred. He sought the truth — in the Bible, and in his own mind. The geologist seeks some of the same truth in the rocks; the astronomer in the stars. The Old Testament was this scholar's field. And, laying aside tradition and the spirit of dogma, he sought as a scientist seeks, patiently, fearlessly, reverently, for what his long and thorough preparation made him eminently able to find.

This is the highest type of courage and daring. Who finds truth finds trial and adventure. In his condemnation by the bishops of his Church, he felt that truth had been assailed and the scientific method. He did not write this book to defend the truth, nor to defend himself; but to examine himself, as he would examine a difficult fragment of Hebrew manuscript, and make himself easy for other men to read.

His trial was long past, and most of his life had been lived, before a page of his book was written. He came at it reluctantly: he might seem personal — petty or selfish or egotistical; or he might say something bitter and vindictive and do harm to the Church. But neither himself nor his Church must stand in the way of truth; and in his trial, truth had been tried, and the only way of knowing truth had been condemned. So he sits down to write this story of his life exactly as he sat down to write a commentary on the Book of Genesis — to account for his being as a man and a scholar, his preparation, his methods of study, his attitude, and approach.

How much truth has he discovered? He makes no claims. Darwin may or may not have the truth about Evolution; but we have a certain and a great truth in Darwin — in his mind and method. It was *how* Darwin tried to solve the problem of life and its forms, rather than the solution, that has changed the thinking of the world.

For three years I was a student of Hebrew and Old Testament Exegesis under this scholar. I have forgotten all he taught me, and more. But the *way* he taught me has changed forever my outlook upon life. His attitude was truth, and it flooded not only the whole mind, but one's whole being, with light. Many a time I have sat in his classroom during the discussion of some highly difficult and dangerous question of doctrine, and said to myself, amid the drawn daggers of those who had come to trap him, "Right or wrong his findings, he is himself truth, its life and way."

Life enough for a book? He could have written a book on teaching. For he loved to teach! He loved to teach young preachers. He could not preach; but he was the teacher born. The classroom was his from the foundation of the world. Here he was preaching truly — from a thousand future pulpits at the very ends of the earth. He saw his students scattered over the whole world preaching to the intelligences of men as well as to their hearts; revealing the wisdom as well as the love of God; and expounding a diviner Bible because it was a wholly human Bible. In all of these pulpits he heard himself speaking with tongues not his own, but the message was his own, the simple sincere faith of his classroom.

The thought of it thrilled him. It lifted him up. He dwelt in the presence of the opportunity as in the very presence of the Most High. As humble a man as ever lived, doubting his every power and gift, and relying only on the truth to make him free, he would come into the classroom and take his chair on the six-inch platform, which raised him by so much above his students, as if that platform were the Mount of Transfiguration. His face would shine; his voice, his gestures, his attitude working with his careful words, made his whole being radiant with zeal for the truth and love for us, his students, so mysteriously given to his care.

Then suddenly, after more than twenty years of this, he was expelled — driven from this sacred classroom and branded as unsound, unsafe, unfit!

No, not suddenly. It was only the verdict of his judges that came suddenly. No one nowadays could prepare his mind for a judgment like that. For five or six of the years, during which the trouble-makers, under pretense of study, had elected his courses at the Theological School, I had either been a student under him or his close and sympathetic friend. I knew, as he knew, that his enemies would stop at nothing in their bitter zeal; still, I remember vividly the utter shock and astonishment of the bishops' decision. And I remember — for I cannot forget — its strange numbing effect upon him. It came over him slowly, else I think he might have died. It crept upon him like a dreadful palsy, leaving him dazed and dumb. He was too simple a man to realize it quickly, too entirely single in mind and heart to realize it wholly. It slowly crushed him to the earth. And never in all the after years was he whole again. His heart was broken. He rose up and taught, until the very hour of his death, but never again in his old classroom nor with his old spirit. Day after day he would pass by the Theological School with its hundreds of eager students; he would see them gathering at the hour of his lecture; but another teacher (one whom he had trained) would come in and take his place, while he plodded down the street and on, a shepherd without his sheep.

Meantime he was called to teach in another graduate school. He welcomed this new work. He found honor, and love, and fellowship among his new colleagues. They gave him freedom. They created a place for him that had not been before. He could teach what he wished and as he wished. It was enough for them to have him among them, and many a time he told me of how unworthy he felt of all this love and honor in his declining years, and how it had stayed and steadied him in his deep defeat. But they did not need him here — so he felt. It was more for the honor of scholarship than for the good he would do them. But he felt that they did need him at his own beloved school, whose policies he had helped to shape, whose spirit he had helped to create, whose name and fame he had so largely helped to establish, and whose students, crowding in from the east and from the great west, he longed to take into his heart and his home, as for so many happy years he had been in the habit of doing.

"O Jerusalem, Jerusalem," he would cry as he passed by on the street, a stranger, and saw the students going in and out, "O Jerusalem, Jerusalem, which killeth the prophets, . . . how often would I have gathered thy children together, even as a hen gathereth her chickens under her wings, and ye would not!"

This, however, was not the doing of the school. Faculty and students, with the exception of those few who came for the express purpose of accusing him, were loyal. The president of the University, his close friend, was loyal, and did all that lay in his power to prevent the iniquity of the trial and the decision. This only added to the tragedy. To have been tried by his peers and co-laborers, by those who knew him and the field of his labors, would have been perfectly fair, but to be accused by three or four narrow-minded students (one of whom recanted later and all of whom deserve oblivion), who had come with malice aforethought, whose very presence in the school was a lie, to be accused by such as these, I say, and then tried by a board of judges, to whom he was largely a stranger, not one of whom probably was his equal as a scholar in the field involved — this made the shame to the school, to himself, and to truth, doubly deep and sore.

There remained one thing more for him to do; and as soon as he could do it kindly, as a Christian, and dispassionately, as a scholar, without bias or prejudice or any personal ends except the ends of gratitude and truth, he set about his autobiography. And I wonder if, among autobiographies, there is another that approaches his for detachment, restraint, and self-negation; for absolute adherence to the facts for the sake of the truth involved, a truth not of self at all, but wholly of scholarship? This is more of a thesis than an autobiography — as if the author were writing of another "Wall of Nehemiah," and no more involved in it, personally, than he was present in "The World before Abraham"!

This is one of the most remarkable evidences of severe and scientific scholarship that I have ever seen; and it is equal evidence of the inherent literary value of human life. No accusing word is here, nothing bitter and unchristian. But just the opposite: "For the Benefit of My Creditors" is a work of love. His very character had been assailed by his enemies, but this, while it hurt, could not harm him. He stood upon his conscious integrity, calm and silent. It was not the attack upon himself that concerned him. It was that Truth had been attacked. It was an attempt to make the Bible a denominational book; to confound truth with tradition and give it a doctrinal color or a denominational slant. The Church may compel its *theologians* to do that if it has to, but its scholars, those who discover truth, it should leave free. God and truth are not denominational, nor Protestant nor Catholic nor Hebrew. God is truth, and single or separate, God and Truth belong to the fearless, the frank, and the pure — in science not more than in religion. For "are ye not as the children of the Ethiopians unto me, O children of Israel? . . . Have not I brought up Israel out of the land of Egypt, and the Philistines from Caphtor, and the Syrians from Kir?"

I recall the day we came upon that wonderful passage in Amos in our study of this prophet; and how for the first time in my life the universality of truth dawned upon me out of that passage. I had had a tribal, denominational God, up to that time. I had been seeing different kinds of truth — like the different tribes of old in Palestine — warring truths, each with its own territory, its own grip upon me, when suddenly, as the "Rabbi" opened up this mighty saying of Amos, I saw one God of us all, one truth for us all, and all of us searching, under God's leading, for the truth. Henceforth the Philistines and the Syrians and the children of Israel were to be as the Ethiopians to me, as they are to God — all of us led by him, and all of us free. No teacher ever taught me a diviner lesson than that.

It was not a body of truth that this great teacher was called to expound. It was the spirit of truth — the desire for truth, the search for truth, the nature of truth, *that it is God* — this was his high calling. And in condemning him, his Church was confounding tradition and truth, blocking the road to truth, and threatening, in this example of him, to punish the daring who discover and bring us forward into new realms of truth. In his trial and condemnation the Church was saying: "Study, but study to perpetuate the past; to preserve the old; to defend doctrine, and establish tradition. We have the truth, the whole truth, and nothing but the truth. No new light can possibly break forth from God's word, or from any word. Revelation is closed. And if you think you have new light, hide it, and if you discover new truth, do not publish it, do not teach it, for among the three hundred men in your school there are three who have closed their minds to light and truth, and have sworn by all the past to keep them closed; and it would jeopardize the Church if you should pry those three minds open to the light and to the truth of to-day."

These are not his words. There is a tang of bitterness in them. They are mine. Yet it was partly because he believed that the Church meant to make him a warning to all scholars and honest thinkers within its fold, that he set about his autobiography, which he died writing.

"Rabbi," we students called him affectionately, and strangely enough he seemed to look the part. He was the thorough scholar. Careful, methodical by nature, he was severely trained, and to all of this he added a profound reverence for the Book which was his life's study, and felt a deep sense of his responsibility as its teacher. Had his life's task been a haystack with one single needle of divine truth lost within it, he would have tirelessly taken it down, straw by straw, for the needle of truth, just as Madame Curie, aware of some mysterious power in the crude common bulk of slag, patiently eliminated pound after pound, ton after ton of the gross elements until she held in her hand the pulsing particle of radium, hardly larger than the head of a pin, whose light illumines and almost blinds the groping world. Had Professor Mitchell not been a student of the Bible, he might have been a student of chemistry, for his methods and his zeal were exactly those of the discoverer in any field, and it might have been his honor and glory, as it chanced to be Madame Curie's, to give radium to the world.

Instead of glory, his was condemnation and defeat. Yet his very mind and method, applied anywhere else, would have won him distinction and honor. There is no other mind or method, except the closed mind and the method of appeal to authority, as against the trial by experiment and fact. Truth is truth whether in Theology or in Chemistry, and only the open mind, the free, the bold, the experimenting mind finds it. Traditions have to be defended. Truth is its own defense. The mind of the great scholar is never on the defensive. Let "the Forts of Folly fall," he is far over the frontier where there is no need for forts. So here in his life he writes not to defend himself, but to express himself, his gratitude; and to explain himself, his position, his purpose, his principles as to the way of truth.

Here is a man who was as simple as he was sincere. But simplicity in a great spirit is the sign, the very expression of sincerity. He was interested in all human things. He could make wonderful coffee. He could build a stone wall with the best of masons, and how he used to tramp the woods with me for mushrooms!

I was a stranger in Boston and had been in his classes for a week, perhaps, when I met him downtown. It was a very real pleasure to be stopped and called by name and quizzed by the great Rabbi. What was I looking for in Boston? A hammer? "Come along," he said, turning short about, "there's a good hardware store down this street. I'll go with you and see that you get a Maydole — a Maydole now — they're the only wear in hammers." I got the Maydole; that was twenty-six years ago; I have it yet. His was a little act. But I have drawn many a nail with that hammer. Yea, I have built him a mansion with it.

I speak of that little thing because it was a characteristic act. The details of life tremendously interested him. He was entirely human and as interested in the human side of his students as he was in their intellectual and spiritual sides. From my study window here in Hingham as I write, eight stone faces stare at me out of the retaining wall in the driveway, — big granite chunks of boulder they were in my meadow years ago. It was the Rabbi who rigged the tackle and helped me put those stones here in the wall. He could fix a toggle, he could "cut" and "pize" and "wop" a stone with lever and chain so as to "move mountains." "There!

There!" he would say, "let the mare do the work; let the mare do the work," when I would rush up at a quarter-ton chunk of solid granite and, bare-handed, try to hustle it on to the stone-boat.

He had built stone walls before — back on the hill farm in New York State, where he was born and had his boyhood. Later he "restored" the Wall of Nehemiah about Jerusalem, but not with any more zest than he helped me build with actual stones the retaining wall for my driveway up Mullein Hill in Hingham. Such is the man. Would he be substance for a book?

Theological students are as naturally full of trouble as rag-weeds are of pollen. They know enough to doubt; they are old enough to be married; they are poor; and they preach; and they would like to be pious; but the world and the flesh and the devil are against them. They are only as good as the average of mankind, but they have more than an average share of tribulations. They need Hebrew — all of them — which is one more terrible trouble! But they sorely need human sympathy and wise counsel, and whether they got Hebrew or failed to get it, never a man came into the Rabbi's classroom who did not also enter at the same moment into his open heart and open home. Classroom and heart and home belonged to every man who would enter. His capacity for patience in the classroom was only equaled by the boundless sympathy and the simple hospitality of his near-by home.

Is it a wonder that the great body of his students were confounded and dismayed that he could be tried on some technical point or other and be ejected from his chair as unfit to teach those who were to preach the Gospel?

After the trial the enforced leisure was immediately turned to new studies and larger literary plans. Fresh fields were opened, too, for lecturing — in the University of Chicago, in Harvard University; and then soon came the invitation to join the staff of Tufts Theological School as a member of the faculty. Life has its compensations and rewards; and if there was no cure for the mortal wound he had received at the hands of his brethren in his own Church, this invitation to Tufts, and the perfect fellowship there to the day he died, was a compensation and a satisfaction that gave to his life a sweet reasonableness, completeness, and reward.

There was no variableness nor shadow caused by turning in his unhurried life. The loss of his chair did not mean the end of his creative scholarship. He worked to the last, and was preparing for the day's work when death came. He knew our hearts, but we ourselves hardly knew them till he had gone. Then the swift word reached us, and we were told that we should see him no more, that he was to be buried afar with no service of any kind for him here — here where he had labored so many years! It could not be. On every hand his old pupils appeared — Methodist, Universalist, Unitarian — in one mind, all differences forgotten in their single love for the honest scholar, the direct, the earnest, the sincere teacher, the simple man, whose life had been devoted to learning and to doing good, — on every hand they appeared and gave him "The Grammarian's Funeral."

"Thither our path lies; wind we up the heights!
Wait ye the warning?
Our low life was the level's and the night's:
He's for the morning.

Step to a tune, square chests, erect each head,
'Ware the beholders!
This is our master, famous, calm, and dead,
Borne on our shoulders.

"This, throws himself on God, and unperplexed
Seeking shall find him.
So, with the throttling hands of death at strife,
Ground he at grammar;
Still, through the rattle, parts of speech were rife:
While he could stammer
He settled *Hoti's* business — let it be! —
Properly based *Oun* —
Gave us the doctrine of the enclitic *De*,
Dead from the waist down.

"Here's the top-peak; the multitude below
Live, for they can, there:
This man decided not to Live but Know —
Bury this man there?
Here — here's his place, where meteors shoot,
clouds form,
Lightnings are loosened,
Stars come and go! Let joy break with the storm,
Peace let the dew send!
Lofty designs must close in like effects:
Loftily lying,
Leave him — still loftier than the world suspects,
Living and dying."

CHAPTER VI
A JANUARY SUMMER

CHAPTER VI

A JANUARY SUMMER

When winter winds blow cold and chill
And through the hawthorn howls the gale

THE winter winds were truly cold and chill on this twenty-first of January here in Massachusetts. And I chance to know they were chill down along the Delaware this particular January day. I remember many a January day like this on the wide marshes of the Delaware and in the big woods along the Maurice River where I was a boy. But I was not thinking of those days at all here in my New England home, for I was busy at my desk.

Some one was at my study door. More than one, for I heard low talking. Then the door softly opened, and four bebundled boys stood before me — with an axe, a long-handled shovel, a covered basket, and a very big secret, which stuck out all over their faces.

They were not big boys outside. But they were almost bursting inside with their big secret. They were big with boots and coats and caps and mittens; and they looked almost like monsters in my study door with their axe and shovel and big basket.

"Come on, father," they whispered (as if *She* hadn't heard them tramping through the hall and upstairs with their kit!), "come on! It's mother's birthday to-morrow, and we're going after the flowers."

"What!" I exclaimed. "Are you going to chop the flowers down with an axe, and dig them up with a shovel?" And I tried to think what a chopped-down and dug-up birthday bouquet would look like. But it was too much for me.

"You are going to give her a nice bunch of frost flowers," I said, feeling about in my puzzled mind for just what was afoot. "If you are going to give her frost flowers, you had better get the ice-saw, too, for we shall need a big block of ice to stick their stems in."

Not a word of comment! No sign on the four faces that they had even heard my gentle banter. They knew what they were going to do; and all they wanted of me was to come along.

"Hurry up," they answered, dropping my

hip-boots on the floor. "Here are your scuffs."

I hurried up! Scuffs and boots and cap and reefer on in a jiffy, and the five of us were soon in single file upon the meadow, the dry snow squealing under our feet, while the little imp-winds, capering fitfully about us, blew the snow-dust into our faces, or catching up the thin drifts, sent them whirling and waltzing, like ghostly dancers, over the meadow's level glittering floor.

I was beginning to warm up a little; but I was still guessing about the flowers, and not yet in the spirit of the game.

We were having a hard winter, and the novelty of zero weather was beginning to wear off — at least to me. The fact was I had intended to get the birthday flowers down at the greenhouse in the village. January is an awkward time to have a birthday, anyhow. June is a much more reasonable month for birthdays, if you gather wild flowers for the celebration. The fields are full of flowers in June! But here in January you must go with an axe and a shovel, mittens, rubber-boots, and reefers! And I confess I couldn't make head or tail of this festive trip.

It is a lucky man who has boys, or who knows and "trains," as our New Englanders say, with boys. They won't let him freeze up.

"Come, father," they say, "get into your scuffs and boots, and hit the old trail for the woods!" And father drops his pen; bundles up; "clomps" out in his boots, grumbling at the weather and the boys and the birthdays and the stiffness in his knees and in his soul — for a whole hundred yards or more into the meadow! Then he begins to warm up. Then he takes the axe from one of the boys and looks at its edge, and "hefts" it; and looks about for a big birthday flower, about the size of a hundred-year-old oak, to chop down. Something queer is happening to father. He is forgetting his knees; he is capering about on the snow; he is getting ahead of the boys; he hardly realizes it, but he is beginning to feel like a birthday inside of him; and he will soon be in danger of getting this January day mixed up with the days of June!

But not right off. I was warming up, I do confess, yet it was a numb, stiff world about us, and bleak and stark. It was a world that looked all black and white, for there was not a patch of blue overhead. The white underfoot ran off to meet the black of the woods, and the woods in turn stood dark against a sky so heavy with snow as to shut us apparently into some vast snow cave. A crow flapping over drew a black pencil-line across the picture — the one sign of life that we could see besides ourselves. Only small boys are likely to leave their firesides on such a day; only small boys and those men who can't grow up. Yet never before, perhaps, had boys or men ever gone afield on such a tramp with an axe, a shovel, and a basket.

Suddenly one of the boys dashed off calling, "Let's go see if the muskrats have gone to bed yet!" And trailing after him away we went, straight across the meadow. I knew what he was after; I could see the little mound, hardly more than an anthill in size, standing up in the meadow where the alder bushes and elderberry marked the bend in the brook. If my farmer neighbor had forgotten a small haycock, when he cut his rowen, it would have looked about as this muskrat lodge here buried under the snow. I was glad the boys had seen it. For only a practiced eye could have discovered it; and only a lover of bleak gray days would have known what might be alive deep down under its thatch of cat-tails and calamus here in the silent winter.

But is there any day in the whole year out of doors that real live boys and real live girls do not love? or any wild thing that they do not love — flower or bird or beast or star or storm?

We crept up softly, and surrounded the lodge; then with the axe we struck the frozen, flinty roof several ringing blows. Instantly *one* — *two* — *three* muffled splashy "plunks" were heard, as three little muskrats, frightened out of their naps and half out of their wits, plunged into the open water of their doorways from off their damp but cozy couch.

It was a mean thing to do, but not very mean as wild animal life goes. And it did warm me up so, in spite of the chilly plunge the little sleepers took! Chilly to them? Not at all, and that is why it warmed me. To hear the splash of water down under the two feet of ice and snow that sealed the meadow like a sheet of steel! To hear the sound of stirring life, and to picture that snug, steaming bed on the top of a tough old tussock, with its open water-doors leading into freedom and plenty below! "Why, it won't be long before the arbutus is in bloom," I began to think. I looked at the axe and shovel, and said to myself, "Well, the boys may know what they are doing, after all, though three muskrats don't make a spring or a bouquet."

But they did make me warmer inside and outside, too. Warm up your heart and you soon feel warmer in your fingers and toes.

We turned back from the muskrats' lodge and headed again for the woods, where the flowers must be. Hardly had we reached the cart-path before another of the boys was off — this time to the left, going rapidly toward a low piece of maple swamp perhaps a quarter of a mile away.

"He's going over to see if Hairy Woodpecker is in his hole," said the boys in answer to my question. "Hairy has a winter hole over there in a big dead maple. Want to see him?"

Of course I wanted to see him. The only live thing outside of ourselves that we had seen (we had only *heard* the muskrats) had been a crow. Live birds on such days as these one would go far to see. So we all cut across toward the swamp where the hairy woodpecker reigned solitary in his bleak domain.

The "hole" was almost twenty-five feet up in a dead maple stub that had blown off and lodged against a live tree. The meadow had been bleak and wind-swept, but the swamp was naked and dead, filled with ice, and touched with a most forbidding emptiness and stillness. I was getting cold again, when the boy ahead tapped lightly on the old stub. At the hole upstairs appeared a head — a fierce black-and-white head, a sharp, long bill, a flashing eye — as Hairy came forth to fight for his castle. He was too wise a fighter to tackle all of us, however; so, slipping out, he spread his wings, and galloped off with a loud wild call that set all the swamp to ringing.

It was a thrilling, defiant challenge that set my blood to leaping again. Black and white, he was a part of the picture; but there was a scarlet band in the nape of his neck that, like his call, had fire in it and the warmth of life.

As his shout went booming through the hollow walls of the swamp, it woke a blue jay, which squalled back from a clump of pines, then, wavering out into the open on curious wings — flashing ice-blue and snow-white wings — he dived into the covert of pines again; and faint, as if beyond the swamp, the cheep of chickadees!

If anything was needed up to this moment to change my winter into spring, it was this call of the chickadees. The dullest day in winter smiles; the deepest, darkest woods speak cheerfully to me, if a chickadee is there. And did you ever know a winter day or a dank, gloomy forest hall without its chickadee? Give me a flower in my buttonhole and a chickadee in my heart and I am proof against all gloom and cold.

"What is all this noise about?" the chickadees came forward asking. It was a little troop of them, a family of them, possibly, last year's children and one, or both, of the parents, hunting the winter woods together for mutual protection against the loneliness and long bitter cold.

How active and interested in life they were! A hard winter? Yes, of course, but what is the blue jay squawking over, anyhow? And the little troop of them came to peep into the racket, curious, but not excited, discussing the disturbance of the solemn swamp in that sewing-bee fashion of theirs, as if nipping off threads and squinting through needle-eyes between their running comments.

They too were gray and black, gray as the swamp beeches, black as the spotted bark of the birches. And how tiny! But —

> "Here was this atom in full breath
> Hurling defiance at vast death;
> This scrap of valor just for play
> Fronts the north wind in waistcoat gray";

and this is what Emerson says he sings:

> "Good day, good sir!
> Fine afternoon, old passenger!
> Happy to meet you in these places
> Where January brings few faces."

And as I brought to mind the poet's lines, I forgot to shiver, and quite warmed again to the idea of flowers, especially as one of the boys just then brought up a spray of green holly with a burning red berry on it.

I laid the spray of green holly on the hard white crust of the January snow. Then I stood a moment and spread my hands out over it to warm them! It was like a little fire in the snow. The boys laughed at me. They were warm enough in their mittens. But I had need of more than mittens to warm my fingers. I had need of a fire, — a fire of green pointed holly leaves and one glowing, flaming berry, a tiny red hot coal of summer blazing here in the wide white ashes of the winter.

We were tacking again now in order to get back on our course, and had got into the edge of the swamp among the pines when the boy with the shovel began to study the ground and the trees as if trying to find the location of something.

"Here it is," he said, and began digging through the snow at the foot of a big pine. I knew what he was after. It was goldthread, and here was the only spot in all the woods about where we had ever found it, a spot no larger than the top of a dining-room table.

Soon we had a fistful of the delicate plants with their evergreen leaflets and long golden, threadlike roots that, mixed with the red and green of the partridge-berry in a finger-bowl, make a cheerful winter bouquet. And here with the goldthread, about the butt of the pine, was the partridge-berry, too, the dainty vines strung with the beads which seemed to burn holes in the snow that covered and banked their tiny fires.

For this is all that the ice and snow had done. The winter had come with enough wind to blow out every flame in the maple-tops, and with enough snow to smother every little fire in the peat-bogs of the swamp; but peat fires are hard to put out; and here and everywhere the winter had only banked the fires of summer. Dig down through the snow ashes anywhere, and the smouldering coals of life burst into blaze.

When that red-beaded partridge-vine was hastily placed with the goldthread in the covered basket, and the spray of holly put with them, a ray of light began to dawn on my snow-clouded mind. Did I begin to see the bouquet these boys were after? I said nothing. They said nothing. They were watching me, though, I knew, to see how long I should stumble blindly on through these glorious January woods, which were so full of joy for them.

I say I said nothing. I was thinking hard, however. "Holly, goldthread, partridge-berry," I thought to myself. "I see so much of the birth-day bouquet. But what else can they find?"

The boy with the axe had again gone on ahead. And we were off again after him, stopping to get a great armful of black alder branches that were literally aflame with red berries.

We were climbing a piny knoll when almost at our feet, jumping us nearly out of our skins, and warming the very roots of our hair, was a burrrr! burrrr! burrrr! burrrr! — four big partridges — as if four snow-mines had exploded under us, hurling bunches of brown feathers on graceful scaling wings over the dip of the hill!

This was getting livelier all the time. From my study window how dead and deserted, and windswept and bare the world had looked to me! Nothing but a live crow winging wearily against the leaden sky! But out here in the real woods and meadows — partridges, chickadees, hairy woodpecker, blue jay, and muskrats as well as crows! And then I knew a certain old apple tree where a pair of screech owls were wintering. And, as for white-footed mice, I could find them in any stump. Besides, here were rabbit holes in the snow, and up in a tall pine a gray squirrel's nest and —

But I was losing sight of the boy with the

axe who was leading the procession. On we went up over the knoll and down into a low bog where in the summer we gathered high-bush blueberries, the boy with the axe leading the way and going straight across the ice toward the middle of the bog.

My eye was keen for signs, and I soon saw he was heading for a sweet-pepper bush with a broken branch. My eye took in another bush a little to the right also with a broken branch. The boy with the axe walked up to the sweet-pepper bush, and drew a line on the ice between it and a bush off on the right, pacing off this line till he found the middle; then he started at right angles from it, and paced off a line to a clump of cat-tails sticking up through the ice on the flooded bog. Halfway back on this line he stopped, threw off his coat, and began to chop a hole about two feet square in the ice. Removing the block of ice while I looked on, he rolled up his sleeve, and reached down the length of his arm through the ice water.

"Give me the shovel," he said, "it's down here." And with a few dexterous cuts he soon brought to the surface a beautiful cluster of pitcher-plants, the strange, almost uncanny, leaves filled with muddy water, but every pitcher of them intact, shaped and veined and tinted by a master potter's hand.

Now at last I fully understood. Now I could see what those boys had been seeing with their inward eyes all the time. Now I had faith, too. But how late! The bouquet of flowers was now full.

We wrapped the wonderful pitcher-plant carefully in newspapers, and put it into the basket, starting back with our bouquet as cheerfully, and as full of joy in the season, as we could possible have been in June.

No, I did not say that we love January as much as we love June. January here in New England is a mixture of rheumatism, chilblains, frozen water-pipes, mittens, overshoes, blocked trains, and automobile-troubles by the hoodsful, whereas any automobile will run in June. It is so in Delaware and Texas and Oregon, too.

What I was saying is that we started home all abloom with our pitcher-plants and goldthread and partridge-berry and holly and glowing black alder, and all aglow inside with our vigorous tramp, and with the gray grave beauty of the landscape, and with the stern joy of meeting and beating the cold, and with the signs of life — of the cozy muskrats in their lodge beneath the ice-cap on the meadow; with the hairy woodpecker in his deep warm hole in the heart of a tree; with the red warm berries in our basket; with the chirping, the capable, the conquering chickadee accompanying us and singing,

> "For well the soul, if stout within,
> Can arm impregnably the skin;
> And polar frost my form defied,
> Made of the air that blows outside."

And actually as we came over the bleak meadow, one of the boys said that he thought he heard a song-sparrow singing! And I said I thought the pussy-willows by the brook had opened a little since we had passed them coming out! And we all declared that the weather had changed, and that there were signs of a break-up. But the thermometer stood at fifteen above zero when we got home — one degree colder than when we started!

We had had a January thaw, however, and it had come off inside of us, as the color on the four glowing faces showed. The birthday came off on the morrow, and I wonder if there ever was a more interesting or a more loving gift of flowers than those from the January woods?

CHAPTER VII

AFTER THE LOGGERS

CHAPTER VII

AFTER THE LOGGERS

I LAY listening to the rain spattering against the fly of the tent and dripping through the roof of birch leaves upon the sputtering fire and soaking down into the deep, spongy bottom of the forest — softly, as soft as something breathing and asleep. The guide and the boy beside me were asleep, but I had been awakened by the rain. The rain always wakens me. And in my grave, I think, if I lie sleeping under a roof of forest leaves, I shall wake and listen when it rains. Before the stars sang together the primordial waters made music to the rising land; before the winds came murmuring through the trees the waves were fingering the sweet-tuned sands strung down the sounding shores; and before the birds found their tongues, or the crickets their little fiddles, or even the toad had blown his quavering conch, it had rained! And when it rained — and not until it rained — the whole earth woke into song. Mother of music is the water, and, for me, the sweetest of her daughters is the rain, and never sweeter, not even on the shingles, nor down the rolled, fevered blades of the standing corn, than in the deep woods at night upon the low slant roof of your tent.

But suddenly the singing stopped, and the myriad rain-notes were turned to feet, tiny, stirring feet, creeping down the tent, skipping across the leaves, galloping over the forest floor, and jumping in and out of the fire. Then a twig snapped. Was that what had awakened me? I rose up on my elbow slowly. The tent flap was open; the woods were very dark, the dim light from above the roof of leaves and rain showing only shadows, and an ashen spot where the camp-fire still spluttered, and beyond the ashen spot a shadow — different from the other shadows; a shape — a doe with big ears forward toward the fire! A bit of birch bark flared in the darkness, and the shape was gone. I could hear her moving through the ferns; hear her jump a fallen log and step out among the grating pebbles on the shore. Then all was still, except for the scampering rain, and the little red-backed wood-mouse among the camp tins, and the teeth of a porcupine chilled and chattering in the darkness at the big wood-mouse among the tins, and the rain running everywhere.

I dropped back upon my pillow and left off listening. How good the duffle-bag felt beneath my head! And the thick, springy bows of the fir beneath the bag, how good they felt — springs and mattress in one, laid underside up, evenly, and a foot deep, all over the tent floor! And how good they smelled! A bed of balsam-fir boughs is more than a bed; it is an oblation to Sleep, and not a vain oblation — after miles of paddling in live water or a day of trailing through the spruce and fir.

> "There's a long, long trail a-winding"

runs the song —

> "Into the land of my dreams."

But, speaking of sleep, there is no trail, except a forest trail, that winds away to a land of such deep dreamlessness as that of a woodman's sleep; and no sleep, from which a man will waken, half so fragrant and refreshing as his. I do not wish to be carried to the skies "on flowery beds of ease," but I should like this balsam-fir bed, for two or three weeks every summer, in the woods of Maine. A reasonable and a wholesome wish that, as I lay there wrapped in the fragrant mantle of my couch, I coveted for city sleepers everywhere.

The odors (we should spell them with a "u") — the od*ou*rs of the big woods are so clean and pure and prophylactic! They clear the clogged senses, and keep them in a kind of antiseptic bath, washing a coated tongue as no wine can wash it; and tingling along the most snarled of nerves, straightening, tempering, tuning them till the very heart is timed to the singing of the firs. My bed of boughs was a full foot deep, covering every inch of the bottom of the tent, fresh cut that evening, and so bruised with the treading as we laid them that their smell, in the close, rainy air of the night, filled the tent like a cloud. I lay and breathed — as if taking a cure, this tent being the contagious ward of the great hospital, the Out-of-Doors. All around me poured the heavy, penetrating vapor distilled from the gums, and resins, and oils, and sweet healing essences of the woods, mingled here in the tent with the aromatic balsam of the fir. I breathed it to the bottom of my lungs; but my lungs were not deep enough; I must breathe it with hands and feet to get it all; but they were not enough. Then a breeze swept by the tent, pausing to lay its mouth over my mouth, and, catching away my little breath, breathed for me its own big breath, until my very bones, like the bones of the birds, were breathing, and every vein ran redolent of the breath of the fir.

That breeze blew the sharp, pungent smell of wood smoke past the tent. I caught it eagerly — the sweet smoke of the cedar logs still smouldering on the fire. There was no suggestion of hospitals in this whiff, but camps, rather, and kitchens, altars, caves, the smoke of whose ancient fires is still strong in our nostrils and cured into the very substance of our souls.

I wonder if our oldest racial memory may not be that of fire, and if any other form of fire, a coal off any other altar, can touch the imagination as the coals of a glowing camp-fire. And I wonder if any other odor takes us farther down our ancestral past than the smell of wood smoke, and if there is another smoke so sweet as cedar smoke, when the thin, faint wraith from the smouldering logs curls past your tent on the slow wind of the woods and drifts away.

It does not matter of what the fire is built. I can still taste the spicy smoke of the sagebrush in my last desert camp. And how hot that sagebrush fire! And as sweet as the spicy sage is the smell in my nostrils of the cypress and gum in my camp-fires of the South. Swamp or desert or forest, the fire is the lure — the light, the warmth, the crackle of the flames, and the mystic incense of the smoke rising as a sweet savor to the deities of the woods and plains.

It is the camp-fire that lures me to the woods when I might go down to the sea. I love the sea. Perhaps I fear it more; and perhaps I have not yet learned to pitch my tent and build my fire upon the waves; certainly I have not yet got used to the fo'c's'le smell. For, of all foul odors known to beast or man, the indescribable stench of the fo'c's'le is to me the worst. What wild wind of the ocean can blow that smell away? When bilges are sprayed with attar of roses, and fo'c's'les sheathed in sandalwood, and sailors given shower-baths and open fires, I shall take a vacation before the mast; but until then give me the woods and my fir-bough bed, and my fire of birch and cedar logs, and the rain upon my tent.

When I woke at dawn it was still raining; and off and on all day it rained, spoiling our plans for the climb up Spencer Mountain and keeping us close to camp and the drying fire. The forest here at the foot of the mountain was a mixed piece of old-growth timber, that had been logged for spruce and pine some years before — as every mile of the forest of Maine has been logged — yet so low and spongy was the bottom that the timber seems to have overgrown and long since ceased to be fit for lumber, so that most of it was left standing when the lumber-jacks went through. We were camped by the side of Spencer Pond in the thick of these giant trees — yellow birch, canoe birch, maple and spruce, hemlock and fir and pine — where the shade was so dense and the forest floor so strewn with fallen trees that only the club mosses, and the sphagnum, and a few of the deep-woods flowers could grow. The rain made little difference to my passage here, so low were these lesser forest forms under the perpetual umbrage of the mighty trees, and I came back from as far in as I dared to venture on so dull a day, my clothes quite dry, but my spirit touched with a spell of the forest, which I should have missed had the sun been shining and the points of the compass clear.

For in the big woods one is ever conscious of direction, a sense that is so exaggerated in the deepest bottoms, especially when only indirect, diffused light fills the shadowy spaces, as to border on fear. I am never free, in a strange forest, from its haunting Presence; so close to it that I seem to hear it; seem able to touch it; and when, for a moment of some minor interest or excitement, I have forgotten to remember and, looking up, find the Presence gone from me, I am seized with sudden fright. What other panic comes so softly, yet with more terrible swiftness? And once the maze seizes you, once you begin to meet yourself, find yourself running the circle of your back tracks, the whole mind goes to pieces and madness is upon you.

"Set where you be and holler till I come get ye, if ye're lost," the guide would say. "Climb a tree and holler; don't run around like a side-hill gouger, or you're gone."

I do not know what sort of animal is Johnny's side-hill gouger; though I saw, one day, far up on the side of the mountain a big bare spot where he had been digging — according to the guide. It is enough for me that there is such a beast in the woods, and that he gets those who turn round and round in the forest on rainy days and forget to look up.

The gouger was abroad in the woods to-day. The clouds hung at the base of the mountains, just above the tops of the trees; the rain came straight down; the huge fallen trunks lay everywhere criss-cross; and once beyond the path to the spring the semi-gloom blurred every trail and put at naught all certainty of direction.

But how this fear sharpened the senses and quickened everything in the scene about me! I was in the neighborhood of danger, and every dull and dormant faculty became alert. Nothing would come from among the dusky trees to harm me; no bear, or lynx, or moose, for they would run away; it was the dusk itself, and the big trees that would not run away; and I watched them furtively as they drew nearer and nearer and closed in deeper about me. I knew enough to "set down and holler" if I got turned hopelessly around; but this very knowledge of weakness, of inability to cope alone with these silent, sinister forces, woke all my ancient fears and called back that brood of more than fabled monsters from their caves and fens and forest lairs.

This was the real woods, however, deep, dark, and primeval, and no mere fantasy of fear. It looked even older than its hoary years, for the floor was strewn with its mouldering dead, not one generation, but ages of them, form under form, till only long, faint lines of greener moss told where the eldest of them had fallen an æon since and turned to earth. Time leaves on nothing its failing marks so deeply furrowed as upon men and trees, and here in the woods upon no other trees so deeply as upon the birches. Lovely beyond all trees in their shining, slender youth, they grow immeasurably aged with the years, especially the yellow birch, whose grim, grizzled boles seemed more like weathered columns of stone than living trees.

One old monster, with a hole in his base that a

bear might den in, towering till his shoulders overtopped the tallest spruce, stood leaning his gnarled hands upon the air, as a bent and aged man leans with his knotty hands upon a cane. A hundred years he might have been leaning so; a hundred years more he might continue in his slow decline, till, with a crash, he falls to lie for a hundred years to come across a prostrate form that fell uncounted years before.

I was standing on the tough, hollow rind of such a birch, so long, long dead that its carcass had gone to dust, leaving only this empty shell that looked like a broken, half-buried piece of aqueduct. It was neither tree nor pipe, however, but the House of Porcupines, as I could plainly hear by the grunting inside. A pile of droppings at the door of the house told the story of generations of porkies going in and out before the present family came into their inheritance. I knocked on the rubbery walls with my foot, but not hard, for I might break through and hurt Mother or Father Porky, or possibly the baby that I saw along the pond that night. No careful, right-minded person steps on or hurts a porcupine in any manner.

I went on out of the sound of their teeth, for chattering teeth are not consoling, and the woods were gray enough. Gray and vast and magnificently ruinous, yet eternally new they were, the old walls slowly crumbling, and over them, out of their heaped disorder, the fresh walls rising to the high-arched roof that never falls. To-day the deep, hollow halls were shut to me by the arras of the gloom, and so smoky rolled the rain beneath the roof that even the black rafters of the birches were scarcely visible; but all the closer about me, in the wildest wealth and splendor, lay the furniture of the forest floor.

Never were wools dyed and woven with a pile so rich and deep as the cover of mosses and lichens that carpeted this rude, cluttered floor. Rolled and wrinkled and heaped up over the stumps, it lay, nowhere stretched, nowhere swept, a bronze and green and gold ground, figured and flowered endlessly; and down the longest, deepest wrinkle a darkling little stream! It was a warp of sphagnum moss with woof of lichens, liverworts, ferns, mushrooms, club mosses, and shier flowers of the shadows, that was woven for the carpet — long, vivid runners of lycopodium, the fingered sort, or club moss, and its fan-leaved cousin, the ground pine, now in fruit, its clusters of spikes like tiny candelabra standing ready to be lighted all over the floor; and everywhere, on every tree-trunk, stump, and log, and stone the scale mosses, myriads of them, in blotches of exquisite shapes and colors, giving the gray-green tone to the walls as the sphagnums gave the vivid bronze-green to the floor. Down to about the level of my head, the dominant note in the color scheme of the walls, hung the gray reindeer moss, tufts and shreds and pointed bunches of it like old men's grizzled beards. Some of the spruces and twisted cedars were covered with it. Shorter in staple than the usnea of the South, stiffer and lighter in color, it is far less somber and funereal; but a forest bearded with it looks older than time. This moss is the favorite winter food of the moose and caribou and deer, and so clean had the moose and deer eaten it from the trees, up as high as they could reach, that the effect on a clear day was as if a thin gray fog had settled in the forest at an even six-foot level from the ground.

Worked in among the lichens and mosses, quite without design, were the deep-woods flowers — patches of goldthread, beds of foam-flower and delicate wood-sorrel and the brilliant little bunchberry. Wherever the sunlight had a chance to touch the cold, boggy bottom it seemed to set the punk on fire and blaze up into these scarlet berries, stumps and knolls and slopes aflame with them, to burn on through the gloom until they should be smothered by the snow. Twin-flower and partridge-berry were laced in little mats about the bases of the trees; here and there the big red fruit of trillium and the nodding blue berries of clintonia were mixed in a spot of gay color with berries of the twisted stalk, the wild lily-of-the-valley, and the fiery seed-balls of the Indian turnip.

These touches of color were like the effect of flowers about a stately, somber room, for this was an ancient and a solemn house of mighty folk. If the little people came to dwell in the shadow of these noble great they must be content with whatever crumbs of sunshine fell from the heaven-spread table over them to the damp and mouldering floor. There were corners so dark that only the coral orchid and the Indian pipe pushed up through the mat of leaves; and other spots, half open to the sky, where the cinnamon fern and the lady fern waved their lovely plumes, and the wood fern, the beech, the oak, and the crested shield ferns grew together, forced thus to share the scanty light dropped to them from the overflowing feast above.

But I never saw mushrooms in such marvelous shapes and colors and in such indescribable abundance as here. The deep forest was like a natural cavern for them, its cold, dank twilight feeding their elfin lamps until the whole floor was lighted with their ghostly glow. Clearest and coldest burned the pale-green amanita, and with it, surpassingly beautiful in color and design, the egg-topped muscaria, its baleful taper in a splotched and tinted shade of blended orange yellows, fading softly toward the rim. Besides these, and shorter on their stems, were white and green and purple russulas, and great burning red ones, the size of large poinsettia blooms; and groups of brown boletus, scattered golden chanterelles, puff-balls, exquisite coral clusters, and, strangest of them all, like handfuls of frosted fog, the snowy medusa. These last I gathered for my lunch, together with some puff-balls and a few campestris, whose spores, I suppose, may have been brought into the woods with the horses when this tract was lumbered years ago. But I had little appetite for mushrooms. It was the sight of them, dimly luminous in the rain, that held me, their squat lamps burning with a spectral light which filled the dusky spaces of the forest full of goblin gloom.

As I sat watching the uncanny lights there was a rush of small feet down the birch at my back, a short stop just above my head, and a volley of windy talk that might have blown out every elf light in the neighborhood. It was very sudden and, breaking into the utter stillness, it was almost startling. A moose could hardly have made more noise. I said nothing back nor took any notice of him. He could kick up the biggest sort of a rumpus if he wished to, for the woods needed it. I only wondered that he had a tongue, dwelling forever here in this solitude. But a red squirrel's tongue is equal to any solitude, and more than once I have caught him talking against it, challenging the silence of all outdoors, as I have seen small boys challenge each other to a blatting-match.

By and by I turned, and so startled him that he dropped a cluster of green berries from his mouth almost upon my head. It was a large bunch of arbor vitæ berries that he was going to store away, for, though he sleeps much of the winter, he is an inveterate hoarder, working overtime, down the summer, as if the approaching winter were to be seven lean years long.

I was glad he had not obtruded earlier, but now he reminded me properly that it was long past noon, and high time for me to get back to camp. It was later than I thought, for the woods had gradually grown lighter, the rain had almost ceased, and by the time I reached camp had stopped altogether. While we were at supper the sun broke through on the edge of the west and ran the rounded basin of the pond over-full with gold. I stepped down to the shore to watch the glorious closing of the day. The clouds had lifted nearly to the tops of the mountains, where their wings were still spread, feathering the sky with gray for far around; a few fallen plumes lying snowy white upon the dark slopes of the lesser hills; then pouring down the hills into the pond, splashing over the gleaming mountains and up against the sky, burst the flood of golden light with indescribable glory.

"All ready," said the guide, touching me on the arm, and I stepped into the bow of the canoe as he pushed quietly off. An Indian never moved with softer paddle, nor ever did a birch-bark canoe glide off with the ease of this one under the hand of John Eastman, as we moved along in the close shadows of the shore.

The light was passing, but the flush of color still lay on the lovely face of the water with a touch of warmth and life that seemed little less than joy; a serene, but not a solemn joy, for there was too much girlish roundness and freshness to the countenance of the water, too much happiness in the little hills and woods that watched her, and in the jealous old mountain that frowned darkly down. Mine, too, were the eyes of a lover, and in my heart was the lover's pain, for what had I to offer this eternal youth and loveliness?

The prow of the canoe swerved with a telling movement that sent my eyes quick to the shore, to see a snow-shoe rabbit racing down a little cove hard at me, with something — a stir of alder leaves, a sound of long, leaping feet making off into the swamp — that had been pursuing him. It was probably a wildcat that had leaped and missed the rabbit and seen us from within his covert. What lightning eyes and lightning legs, thus to leap and turn together! The rabbit had run almost to the canoe, and sat listening from behind a root at the edge of the water, ears straight up and body so tense with excitement that we nosed along close enough to touch him with a paddle before he had eyes and ears for us. Even then it was his twitching, sensitive nose that warned him, for his keen ears caught no sound; and, floating down upon him thus, we must have looked to his innocent eyes as much like a log or a two-headed moose as like men.

Softly in and out with the narrow fret of shadow that hemmed the margin of the pond swam the gray canoe, a creature of the water, a very part of our creature selves, our amphibious body, the form we swam with before the hills were born. Brother to the muskrat and the beaver, I stemmed along, as much at home as they among the pickerel-weed and the cow-lilies, and leaving across the silvery patches of the open water as silent a wake as they.

Nothing could move across such silvery quiet without a trail. So stirless was the water that the wake of a feeding fish was visible a hundred yards away. Within the tarnished smooches of the lily-pads a muskrat might move about and not be seen; but not a trout could swirl close to the burnished surface of the open water without a ripple that ran whispering into every little inlet around the shore. The circle of the pond was almost perfect, so that I roved, at a glance, the whole curving shore-line, watching keenly for whatever might come down to feed or drink.

We came up to a patch of pickerel-weed and frightened a brood of half-grown sheldrakes that went rushing off across the water, kicking up a streak of suds and making a noise like the launching of a fleet of tiny ships. Heading into a little cove, we met a muskrat coming straight across our bows. A dip of the paddle sent us almost into her. A quicker dive she never made nor a more startling one, for the smack as she struck the water jumped me half out of the canoe. Her head broke the surface a dozen yards beyond us, and we followed her into the mouth of a stream and on to a hummock into which she swam as a boat swims under a bridge, or more as a train runs into a tunnel, for an arching hole opened into the mound, just above the level of the stream, through which she had glided out of sight. Hardly had she disappeared before she popped up again from deep under the mound, at the other side, and close to the canoe, starting back once more down-stream. She had dodged us. Her nose and eyes and ears were just above the water and a portion of her back; her bladelike tail was arched, its middle point, only, above the surface, its sheering, perpendicular edges doing duty as propeller, keel, and rudder all at once.

As she made off the guide squeaked shrilly with his lips. Instantly she turned and came back, swimming round and round the canoe, trying to interpret the sounds, puzzled to know how they could come from the canoe, and fearing that something might be wrong inside the house. She dived to find out. By this time two young ones had floated into the mouth of the tunnel, thinking their mother was calling them, blinking there in the soft light so close that I might have reached them with my hand. Satisfied that the family was in order, the old rat reappeared, and no amount of false squeaking would turn her back.

A few bends up the stream and we heard the sound of falling water at the beaver dam. Fresh work had been done on the dam; but we waited in vain for a sight of the workers. They would not go on with their building. One of the colony (there were not more than two families of them, I think) swam across the stream, and came swiftly down to within a few feet of us, when, scenting us, perhaps, he warped short about and vanished among the thick bushes that trailed from the bank of the stream.

A black duck came over, just above our heads, with wings whirring like small airplane propellers, as she bore straight out toward the middle of the pond. We were passing a high place along the shore when a dark object, a mere spot of black, seemed to move off at the side of us against the white line of the pebbles, and I found that I was already being sent silently toward it. My pulse quickened, for the thing moved very slowly; and behind it a lesser blur that also moved — very slowly; so deep was the darkness of the overhanging trees, however, that the nose of the canoe ploughed softly into the sand beside the creatures, and I had not made out the fat old porcupine, and, creeping a foot or two behind her, as if he might catch up by to-morrow, perhaps, the baby porky.

The old mother was feeding on bits of lily-pads washed up along the shore, picking them from among the stones with her paws as if she intended to finish her supper by to-morrow, perhaps, when her baby had covered the foot or two of space between them and caught up with her. She was so intent on this serious and deliberate business that she never looked up as I stopped beside her; she only grunted and chattered her teeth; but I disturbed the baby, apparently, for he speeded up, and pretty soon came alongside his mother, who turned savagely upon him and told him to mind his manners, which he did by humping into a little heap, sticking his head down between two stones, and raying the young quills out across his back in a fan of spines. He didn't budge for about five minutes. Then he hurried again — right up beside the old one — a thing so highly improper in porkypinedom, and so deleterious to porkypine health, that she turned and, with another growl, humped her fat little porky again into a quiet and becoming bunch of quills. This time she read him a lecture on the "Whole Duty of Children." It was in the porcupine-pig language, and her teeth clicked so that I am not sure I got it verbatim, but I think she said, quite distinctly:

"A child should always say what's true,
And speak when he is spoken to,
And behave mannerly at table:
At least as far as he is able" —

for, seeing him so obediently and properly humped, she repented her of her severity and, reaching out with her left paw, picked up a nice, whole lily-pad and, turning half around, handed it to him as much as to say, "There, now; but chew it up very thoroughly, as you did the handle of the carving-knife in the camp last night."

It was a sweet glimpse into the family life of the woods; and as the canoe backed off and turned again down-stream I was saying to myself:

> "Every night my prayers I say,
> And get my dinner every day,
> And every day that I've been good
> I get an orange after food" —

or a nice, round lily-pad.

The precious light was fading, and we had yet more than half the magic circle of the shore to round. As we passed out into the pond again a flock of roosting blackbirds whirred noisily from the "pucker-brush," or sweet-gale bushes, frightened by the squeal of the bushes against the sides of the canoe; and hardly had their whirring ceased when, ahead of me, his head up, his splendid antlers tipped with fire, stood a magnificent buck. He had heard the birds, or had scented us, and, whirling in his tracks, curiosity, defiance, and alarm in every line of his tense, tawny body, stood for one eternal instant in my eye, when, shaking off his amazement, he turned and, bounding over the sweet-gale and alders, went crashing into the swamp.

I had neither camera nor gun; but, better than both, I had eyes — not such good eyes as John Eastman's, for he could see in the dark — but mine with my spectacles were better than a camera; for mine are a moving-picture theater — screen, film, machine, and camera, all behind my spectacles, and this glorious creature for the picture, with the dark hills beyond, the meadowy margin of the pond in the foreground, and over the buck, and the pond, and the dark green hills, and over me a twilight that never was nor ever can be thrown upon a screen!

I had come into the wilds of Maine without so much as a fish-line — though I have fished months of my life away, and am not unwilling to fish away a considerable portion of whatever time may still be left me. But am I not able, in these later days, to spend my time "in the solitude of this vast wilderness with other employments than these, — employments perfectly sweet and innocent and ennobling? For one that comes with a pencil to sketch or sing, a thousand come with an axe or rifle. What a coarse and imperfect use Indians and hunters make of Nature! . . . Strange that so few ever come to the woods to see how the pine lives and grows and spires, lifting its evergreen arms to the light, — to see its perfect success; but most are content to behold it in the shape of many broad boards brought to market, and deem *that* its true success!... Every creature is better alive than dead, men and moose and pine trees, and he who understands it aright will rather preserve its life than destroy it."

Thoreau did not teach me that truth, for every lover of life discovers it himself; but how long before me it was that he found it out, and how many other things besides it he found out here in the big woods! Three-quarters of a century ago he camped on Katahdin, and on Chesuncook, and down the Allegash; but now he camps wherever a tent is pitched or a fire is lighted in the woods of Maine. His name is on the tongue of every forest tree, and on every water; and over every carry at twilight may be seen his gray canoe and Indian guide.

And I wonder, a century hence, who will camp here where I am camping, and here discover again the woods of Maine? For the native shall return. And as "every creature is better alive than dead, man and moose and pine tree"; and as "he who understands it aright will rather preserve *his* life than destroy it" so shall he seek his healing here.

The light had gone out of the sky. It was after nine o'clock. A deep purple had flowed in and filled the basin of the pond, thickening about its margins till nothing but the long chalk-marks of the birches showed double along the shore. The high, inverted cone of Spencer stood just in front of the canoe as we headed out across the pond toward the camp, its shadow and its substance only faint suggestions now, for all things had turned to shadow, the solid substance of the day having been dissolved in this purple flood and poured into the beaker of the night. A moose "barked" off on a marshy point near the dam behind us; a loon went laughing over, shaking the hollow sides of Spencer and all the echoing walls of the woods with his weird and mirthless cry. Against the black base of the mountain a faint bluish cloud appeared — the smoke of our camp-fire that, slowly sinking through the heavy air, spread out to meet us over the hushed and sleeping pond.

CHAPTER VIII

WOODCHUCK LODGE AND LITERATURE

CHAPTER VIII

WOODCHUCK LODGE AND LITERATURE

HAVE I proof of my contention here? Throughout this book, on many sides of the question, I have argued that the earth is as young as it ever was; that Nature, though it can all but be destroyed in spots, as in New York City, cannot be tamed; that we are still the stuff of dreams, if we could find rest for our souls and the chance to dream. We are not lacking imagination and the power for high endeavor. We master material things; we can also handle the raw materials of the spirit and give them enduring form. But how can we come by the raw materials of the spirit? And where shall we find new patterns on which to mould our new and enduring forms? Matter and pattern are still to be found in nature — substance, essence, presence,

> "Whose dwelling is the light of setting suns,
> And the round ocean and the living air,
> And the blue sky, and in the mind of man."

I have had much to do with young people, especially with those of creative minds, divinely capable minds, could they be freed from the doubt of their times, and the fear of their own powers. Here let me give them a glimpse of an *old* man of their own times, these evil times when all of the raw material of books has been used up; an old man with a boy's eyes and a child's heart and a pen and a bluebird or two, and a woodchuck — and, of course, a magical chance.

It was an October day. And how it rained that day! An October day in the Catskills, and I was making my way, with my friend DeLoach, out of the little village of Roxbury by the road that winds up the hills to Woodchuck Lodge. Hardscrabble Creek knew it was raining, and met me noisily at a turn of the road, just before I came to the square stone schoolhouse (now a dwelling) where little Johnny Burroughs had gone for his book learning some seventy-five years before. Leaving the creek, I found myself on a roller-coaster road athwart the hills, making up with spurt and dip to a low, weathered farmhouse, thin and gray and old, that seemed to be resting by the roadside thus far over the mountain on its way to the valley.

I knew it from the distance and through the rain, only it seemed even older, smaller, poorer than I had expected to find it. But how close it sat to the roadside, and how eagerly it gazed down into the valley where the store and the station and the meeting-house were — to see who might be stirring, I thought, down there in the valley! Or perhaps it sat here for the landscape. I was approaching Woodchuck Lodge, and it seemed very old and lonely in the rain that slanted along the wide gray slopes, and too frail to stand long against the pull of the valley and the push of the heights crowding hard upon it from behind.

A tiny kitchen garden at its corner, and across the road a stone wall, an orchard of untrimmed apple trees bent with fruit, and a small barn on the edge of a sharply falling field — this was the picture in the rain, the immediate foreground of the picture, which stood out on a field of hay-lands and pastures rolling out of the rainy sky and down, far down where their stone walls ran into the mists at the bottom of the valley.

These were the ancestral fields. Burroughs was born a little farther along this road, the house no longer standing. Here at the Lodge he was now living, and in the old barn across the road he had a study. These were his fields by right of pen, not plough; these were his buildings, too, and they showed it. They sheltered him and gave him this outlook, but they utterly lacked the pride of the gilded weathervane, the stolid, four-square complacency, that well-fed, well-stocked security of the prosperous American farm. An old pair of tramps were house and barn, lovers of the hills, resting here above the valley. It was in that old barn, on an overturned chicken-coop, with a door or some other thing as humble for table, that Burroughs had written most of the chapters in "The Summit of the Years," in "Time and Change," "The Breath of Life," and "Under the Apple-Trees."

So a literary farm should look, I suppose,—a farm that produces books as abundantly as a prairie farm produces cattle and corn; yet every farm, I think, should have a patch of poetry, as every professional poet certainly needs to keep a garden and a pig. For years Burroughs grew fancy grapes and celery for the New York market, along with his literary essays for the reading public.

As we came in on the vine-covered porch of the Lodge, we were met by Dr. Barrus, Burroughs's physician and biographer, who told us with considerable anxiety that the old man was not at home.

"He is out visiting his traps, I suppose," she said. "He's just like a boy. I can't do anything with him. He'll come home wringing wet. And he's not a bit well."

He came home true to form. It was an hour later, perhaps, that I saw, from the steps, a dim figure in the blur of the rain: an old man plodding slowly down the hill road, a stick and a steel trap in his left hand, and in his right hand a heavy woodchuck.

It was John Burroughs, the real Burroughs, for I knew as I watched him that I had never seen, never clearly seen, this man before — not exactly this simple, rain-soaked man with the snow of more than eighty winters on his head, with the song of eternal springtime in his heart, and a woodchuck, like a lantern, in his hand.

This figure in the rain should be seen coming down every page of Burroughs's books. Every line should be read in the light of this lantern in his hand, for its wick is in his heart, and its flame shines from "Wake-Robin" to "The Summit of the Years." Burroughs was the eternal boy — splashing through the puddles, wet to the skin; the boy for whom these fields of his father's farm were as wild as the jungles of Africa; and this woodchuck in his hand (it *was* a big one!) a very elephant, except for the tusks. But to be like this is to be both boy and philosopher — boy and writer, I should say. And to see him thus — falling with the rain, whirling with the dust, singing with the birds, growing with the grass, his whole being one with the elements, earth and wild-life and weather — thus to see the man is to know how to read his books.

As he came up to the porch, his slouch hat spouting like an eaves-trough, he greeted me cordially, but as a stranger, not recognizing me for an instant; then dashing the rain from his eyes, he dropped the woodchuck, drew off, and with a quick righthander to my chest, which almost took me off my feet, he cried, "Sharp, we'll have woodchuck for dinner!"

And we did — not the one he had just dropped on the floor, for that one he skinned and salted and gave me to bring home to Boston. We had canned woodchuck that noon at the Lodge. It was Burroughs's custom to serve his guests a real literary dinner; and of course it must savor of the locality.

This called for woodchuck, or "Roxbury Lamb," as you preferred; and for roast Roxbury Lamb the rule for rabbit-stew prevails: first get your woodchuck; not always readily done, for the meat-market down at the village is sometimes out of woodchuck. So the Laird of the Lodge keeps them canned ahead.

The clouds cleared in the afternoon, the sun came down upon the mountains, and we looked out from the porch over a world so large and new and lovely that I remember it still as a keen pain, so unprepared was I for it, with my level background of meadow and marsh and bay.

Endless reaches of river and bay, of wavy marshland and hazy barrens of pine, were my heritage of landscape as a child. And I have never been able to measure up to the mountains, nor to this scene, here from the porch — this reach without level; space both deep and high as well as wide; this valley completely hiding a village below you; ridges above you where stone walls climb over the sky; mountains far across with forests flung over their shoulders, and farms, like colored patchwork, stitched into the rents of the forests; runnels singing down the pastures; and roads, your road to school, so close to the verge that only the stone wall stays you from stepping off the edge of the world!

None of this had I known as a boy. "Who couldn't write," I muttered, "born into this glorious world!" I have seen much grander mountains. "Not a rugged, masculine touch in all the view," Burroughs said to me. "It is all sweet and feminine, and doubtless has had a feminizing influence upon my character and writing." It may be so. There is a plenty of wilder, stormier landscape than this in these Western

Catskills, but certainly none that I ever saw that is lovelier for a human home. And here Burroughs now sleeps, under the boulder where he played as a child, and where all this beauty of winding valley and blue, bending sky upon the mountains lies forever about him.

There is something terribly important and lasting about childhood. Almost any environment will do, if only the child is happy. It is the child who counts. In every child the world is recreated and in his memory stays recreated. More and more, as the years lengthen, do we find ourselves longing — for the pine barrens, for the vast green reach of the marshes; and were my feet free this summer day, they would run with my heart to the river — not to the mountains; to the river, the Maurice River, where the bubbling wrens build in the smother of reed and calamus, and where this very day the pink-white marshmallows make, at high noon, a gorgeous sunset over miles of the meadows. I love and understand those great, green levels of marshland as I shall love and understand no other face of nature, it may be. I know perfectly what Lanier means when he sings,

"Oh, what is abroad in the marsh and the terminal sea?
Somehow my soul seems suddenly free
From the weighing of fate and the sad discussion of sin,
By the length and the breadth and the sweep of the marshes
of Glynn."

I said the clouds cleared late that afternoon, but it was still raining when, after dinner, I brought a box from the woodshed to the front porch for Burroughs to skin the woodchuck. Here we sat down together, the flabby, flaccid marmot between us, the whole October afternoon our own.

Burroughs pulled a rudimentary whetstone out of his coat pocket and touched up the blade of his knife — of his spirit, too, running his thumb along the blade of every faculty as he settled to the skinning, his shining eyes, his vibrant voice, his eager movements, all showing how razor-keen an edge the old man was still capable of taking. He got hold of a forefoot of the 'chuck and started to talk on the flight of birds, reviewing the various stages of the controversy on the soaring of hawks that he had been carrying on in the press, when, suddenly dropping his knife, he disappeared through the door and returned in a minute with a letter from some scientist, whose argument, as I remember it, was wholly at variance with Burroughs's theory, but which closed with a strange word, a word the old man had never seen before and could not find in his dictionary. It was some aeronautical term, I think. Handing me the letter, his finger, as well as his eyes, fastened to that stranger from beyond the dictionary, he said:

"That chap doesn't know much about soaring hawks; but there's a new word. See that! He knows a heap more than I do about the English language."

He sat down to the skinning again. No cut had yet been made, nor ever would be made, apparently, unless he used the back of his blade, for it was plain that Burroughs kept that old whetstone for his wits only. He sawed away and talked as if inspired. I held the other forefoot, a short, broad foot, like a side-hill gouger's, on the oldest, toughest 'chuck in the Catskills.

"Do you know what I am going to do?" he asked, switching the conversation into the hard-working knife. "I'm going to pickle this old rascal and send him by you to your family. I want you all to have a dish of 'Roxbury Lamb.'"

"But we have our own Hingham Lamb out on Mullein Hill," I suggested cautiously. "And I don't like to rob you this way."

"No robbery at all. Besides, these are a better breed than yours in Hingham."

"But my folks don't seem very fond of 'em," I protested. "They cook with a rank odor."

"Oh, you don't know how to prepare them," he answered. "Let me show you a trick," and deftly cutting in between the neck and the shoulder, he took out the thyroid glands.

"Now you're going to take this one home. There'll be no strong smell when you cook this fellow."

Our talk turned to poetry — the skinning still going forward — the woodchuck brimming full of verse; for Burroughs, at every other turn of his knife, would seem to open up a vein of song. The beauty of nature to Burroughs had always been more than skin deep. He wanted the skin for a coat; the carcass he wanted for a roast; but here was a chance for him to look into some of the hidden, fearful things of nature, and the sight inside of that woodchuck made him stop and sing.

But how old and frail he looked! And he was old, very old, eighty-four the coming April 9. And he was suddenly sad.

Resting a bit from his labor, he began to chant to the slackening rain:

"'Tis a dull sight
  To see the year dying.
When winter winds
  Set yellow woods sighing,
Sighing, O sighing.

"When such a time cometh,
  I do retire
Into an old room
  Beside a bright fire;
Oh, pile a bright fire!

"I never look out
  Nor attend to the blast,
For all to be seen
  Is the leaves falling fast,
Falling, falling!"

And he rubbed his thin hands together, spread them to the warmth, and repeated two or three times,

"Oh, pile a bright fire!"
"Oh, pile a bright fire!"

More than once, I heard him returning to those lines; and saw him several times reading the last stanzas of the poem from a typewritten copy on his porch table, chafing his hands the while, and extending them before the imaginary fire as if they were cold, or as if he felt through his hands, so sensitive was he physically, an actual fire in the written lines. The poem is Edward Fitzgerald's "Old Song," and I am sure Burroughs was learning it by heart, and making rather hard work of it, I thought, for one who had already in memory so much good poetry. But he was getting very old.

Then, at my request he said some of the lines of his own poem, "Waiting." "The only thing I ever did," he remarked, "with real poetry in it."

"How about the philosophy in it," I inquired, "Do you find it sound after all these years?"

There was an audible chuckle inside of him. Then rather solemnly he replied: "My father killed himself early trying to clear these acres of debts and stones. I might have been in my grave, too, these forty years had I tried to hurry it his way. I waited. By and by Henry Ford came along and cleared up the whole farm for me. Here I am, and here

> "Serene, I fold my hands and wait,
> Nor care for wind, nor tide, nor sea;
> I rave no more 'gainst Time or Fate,
> For lo! my own shall come to me."

We were soon deep in a discussion of free verse, no hungry trout ever rising to the fly with more snap than Burroughs. He called the free-verse writers the Reds of American literature, the figure sticking to him, until some months later in California he worked the idea out into a brief newspaper article under that title, the last piece, I think, for publication from his pen.

"Name me one good modern poem," I said, "moulded on the old forms, with rhyme and meter."

He let go his knife again, turned his face once more to the rain, through which the mountains were now emerging, and asked,

"Do you know Loveman's 'Raining' and how he wandered up from Georgia to find himself in New York City, his boat gone, or his money gone, or something gone — for he was someway stranded, I believe — and it was raining?" And the old man began —

"'It isn't raining rain to me,
It's raining daffodils;
In every dimpled drop I see
Wild flowers on the hills.
The clouds of gray engulf the day,
And overwhelm the town,
It isn't raining rain to me,
It's raining roses down.,'"

while the rain across the hills, shot through with sunset light, fell all violets and clover-bloom and roses on the mountains and on the roof of Woodchuck Lodge.

The thing on the box between us was utterly forgotten, but only for the moment.

"Damn those fleas!" the old poet exploded, at the end of the recitation, swinging with both hands at his long white whiskers, "That 'chuck's alive with fleas!"

So I had observed; and I had been speculating, as I watched them quitting their sinking craft and boarding the sweeping beard of the poet, how many of them it might take to halt the flow of song. I was far off in my reckoning. Burroughs knocked them out and went on:

"That's a good poem because it goes straight to the heart. It's an experience. He lived it. And its form is perfect. You can't change a syllable in it. It's on the old forms, yet it's true to itself. And see how simple, direct, and sincere it is! and how lovely! I call that good poetry."

We had been more than three hours getting the pelt off that woodchuck and all of the poetry out of him. As I sat by, I saw what I had hardly realized before: that the hand with the knife must often rest, though the eager mind seemed almost incapable of resting.

The national elections were approaching, and from poetry we plunged into politics, where I feared we were bound to disagree, but where, to my surprise, I found we were standing together on the League of Nations, Burroughs having forsaken his party on that issue.

"It's the only thing!" he cried. "That's what we fought for. Rob us of that, and the whole terrible sacrifice is futile — criminal!"

And later, after my return home, he wrote me:

"Well, the elections did not go as both of us had hoped. DeLoach was on the winning side, as I suppose all the great moneyed interests were. But thank heaven I am not in that crowd. If it means an utter repudiation of the League of Nations, then for the first time I am ashamed that I am an American. If I were in Europe I could not hold up my head and say, 'I am from the United States!' If we have failed to see ourselves as a member of the great family of nations, with solemn duties toward the rest of the world, to perform as such a member, then we have slumped morally as badly as did the Germans when they set out to enslave the rest of the world!"

But to return to Woodchuck Lodge, to the old man with the boy's jack-knife in his hand, and the boy's heart in his breast — and so, the poet's outlook in his eyes. For he was more poet than scientist, more poet than theologian, though every poet, like all Gaul, is divided into three parts, and these — science, music, and theology — are the parts.

The theologian is the ultimate thinker. His chief attribute is consistency — even unto death.

Nothing will shatter a system of theology as will a trifling inconsistency. Burroughs was a bad theologian, the worst I know by the test of consistency. Yet who among the theologians is more religious? Or leaves us with a realer consciousness of the presence of God in nature?

"You and I approach this thing from different angles," he said to me. "We come to God down different roads. Our terms differ. You say 'Father.' I say 'Nature.' But whatever we call Him, He is the same, and the same for each of us. Our divergent paths at the start, come out together at the end. We worship the same God."

We did differ radically in our approach, in our terminology, and as I had always thought, must of necessity differ as radically in our faiths and works. That was a foolish, vainglorious conceit. I wish every disconcerted reader of "The Light of Day" and "Accepting the Universe" had heard the old author interpret himself that day. That reader would have understood, as he sat there watching the light of a real day breaking in over the rainy autumn landscape, what Carruth meant by,

"A haze on the far horizon,
The infinite tender sky,
The ripe rich tint of the corn-fields,
And the wild geese sailing high,
And all over upland and lowland
The charm of the goldenrod —
Some of us call it Autumn,
And others call it God!"

The pelt was finally off; the carcass in pickle for me; and the sun was out, flooding Montgomery Valley and the heaving ranges beyond. An automobile load of callers came, stopped a little time, and went away; another load came and went away, and Burroughs, now quite rested, brought out the manuscripts of two new books, which were about ready for the publishers.

I looked at the piles of work, then at the frail old man who had heaped them up, and thought with shame of my own strength — and laziness. To be approaching eighty-four with one book on the press and two other books in manuscript! What a long steady stroke he had pulled across these more than sixty years of writing to be bringing him in at the finish, two full volumes ahead of the race! Three volumes indeed, for "Accepting the Universe" had not yet come from the press.

The quiet and calm of it all deeply impressed me. The extreme opposite in temperament and action from his friend Roosevelt, there was nothing "strenuous" about this plodding old man, nor ever had been. "Serene I fold my hands and wait" he had written in his twenty-third year, and had practiced all these four-and-eighty years. Yet look at this amount of durable work accomplished. It is well for us Americans to remember just now that there is another than the "strenuous" type of life, which is just as worthy of emulation, and which is likely to be even more effective.

This was an October day at Woodchuck Lodge. Sixty-one years before the "Atlantic Monthly" was actually printing Burroughs's first essay, "Expression." I looked at the old man beside me with the pen in his fingers. Was it the same man? the same pen? Lowell was the editor; then Fields, Howells, Aldrich, Scudder, Page, Perry, to the present editor, who has held his chair these dozen years; and I watched the pen in Burroughs's hand travel slowly across a corrected line of the manuscript and I remembered that in all the years since Lowell was editor, not for a single year had that pen failed to appear in the pages of the "Atlantic." Was it strange that as I looked from the pen away to the Catskills surrounding me I wondered if I were really looking into Montgomery Valley and not into Sleepy Hollow?

We guests had a plenty that night, but Burroughs went to bed supperless. We guests slept indoors, but Burroughs made his bed out on the front porch, where he could see the stars come over the mountains, and the gates of dawn swing wide on the wooded crests, when the new sweet day should come through and down into Montgomery Valley.

For Burroughs has lived and loved everything he has written. He cannot write of anything else. Our present-day writers, especially our poets and nature writers, take the wings of the morning (or of the night) unto the uttermost parts of the earth for copy. Burroughs visited distant places; but he always wrote about the things at home. "Fresh Fields," to be sure, is out of England; yet England was only an older home. Burroughs had seen strange, extraordinary, tropical things; seen them, to write little about them, however, for it is only the homely, the ordinary, the familiar things that stirred his imagination and moved his pen. These were his things, the furniture of his house, the folks of his town; for it was the hearth where he lived, his home, that he loved, and it was the creatures living on it with him that gave him his great theme. "The whole gospel of my books," he wrote, "is stay at home, see the wonderful and beautiful and the simple things all about you. Make the most of the near at hand."

It was a constant wonder to me how one could be so simple as Burroughs, and yet know so many places, persons, and books. Burroughs had met many people; he had read many books, and had written more than a score himself; yet he was the simplest man I ever knew, as simple as a child, — simpler, indeed. For children may be suspicious and self-conscious, and even uninterested; but Burroughs's interest and curiosity grew with the years. He carried his culture and his knife and his whetstone in his pocket. They belonged to him; but he belonged strictly to himself. He remained to the end what the Lord made him — and that is to be original.

Pietro, the sculptor, has made Burroughs in bronze, resting on a rock, his arm shading his face, his eyes peering keenly into the future or the far-away. Pietro has made him a seer or a prophet. He was much more the lover and the poet. I sat with Burroughs on that same rock, the morning after the rainy day at the Lodge, and talked with him of some things long past, of many things round about us, but of few things of the future. I saw him shield his face with his arm, and look far off from the rock — to the rounded, green-crested hills in the distance, and down into the beautiful valley below. But most of the time he was watching a chipmunk near by, or scanning the pasture for woodchucks. Had I been Pietro I should have made the old man flat on that boulder, his beard a patch of lichen, his slouch hat hard down on his eyes, his head just over the round of the rock — and down the slope, at the mouth of his burrow, a big woodchuck on his haunches.

"I've been studying the woodchuck all my life," he said, as we sat there on the rock, "and there is no getting to the bottom of him."

I do not know whether Burroughs climbed over the walls and up through the field again to this favorite spot of his boyhood in the few remaining days he had at the Lodge. This may have been the last time he looked out with seeing eyes over this landscape of valley and mountain that had been one of the deepest, most abiding influences of his life. As we sat there together, the largeness and glory of the world: colors, contours, the valley depths, the quiet hills, the wealth of life, the full, deep flood of autumn light — almost too much for common human eyes — the old man beside me said, with a sigh:

"I love it. But it is hard to live up to it. Sometimes, especially of late, I feel it a burden too great to bear." Then, as if guilty of some evil thought, he brightened instantly, pointed out a dam that he had built as a boy in the field below us, for his own swimming-hole, the ridge of sod and stone still showing; told me stories of his parents; described his sugar-making in the "bush" behind us; nor referred again to the burden of the years, weighing so heavily now upon him, until we were leaving. Then, as he came out to the road to see us off, he said with tears in his eyes:

"I hate to have you go. I wish you could stay. You boys are life to me now. Come again soon. Good-bye."

We promised we would, and we did — in April, the next April, when we went up to say our last good-bye. Meantime he was off to California for the winter months. Before leaving he wrote to me from West Park, his home on the Hudson:

> I neglected to make any apologies for the long letter I wrote you the other day. I promise not to do so again. I am sending you an old notebook of mine, filled with all sorts of jottings, as you will see. I send it as a keepsake.
>
> We are off for California to-morrow. Hope to be there in early December. We leave Chicago on the 29th. My address there will be La Jolla, San Diego. Good luck to you and yours.
>
> Ever your friend
>
> JOHN BURROUGHS

He kept his promise. This was his last letter to me. They were not very happy months in

California. Visitors came to see him as usual; he spoke in the schools; and wrote up to the very end; but he was weak, often sick, and always longing for home. He knew if he was ever to see home again he must not delay long; and he counted the days. He wished to celebrate his birthday with his old friends, at the old place; and he was on the way, speeding homeward, with most of the long journey covered, when, suddenly, the end came. And is it at all strange that his last uttered words, as he sank into unconsciousness, should have been "How far are we from home?"

On the front of the boulder which marks his grave, those last words might well be cut, as expressing the real theme of all his books, the dominant note in all his life.

His old friends kept his birthday in the old place — in the "Nest" at Riverby, for the funeral; and the next day, his eighty-fourth birthday, they carried him into his beloved mountains, to his grave by the rock, where so lately we had talked together, and where, since childhood, he had found an altar for his soul.

How great a man Burroughs was I do not

know. Time knows. I know that he had three of the elements of greatness as a writer: simplicity, sincerity, and a true feeling for form. And he had these to an uncommon degree. I know that great men and little children loved him; and that three generations already have been led oftener and farther into the out-of-doors by him than by any other American writer. I know how Burroughs thought of himself and of Thoreau; for in a letter, several years ago to me he wrote:

> Thoreau is nearer the stars than I am. I may be more human, but he is as certainly more divine. His moral and ethical value I think is much greater, and he has a heroic quality that I cannot approach.

But I am not trying to estimate Burroughs. I am only sketching, through the gray rain and in the golden light at the far end of the autumn, one whom thousands of us read and love.

THE END